Panaghiótis Chrístou - Katharini Papastamatis

# GODS AND HEROES IN
# GREEK
# MYTHOLOGY
## THE TROJAN WAR AND THE ODYSSEY

**BONECHI**

*Project and editorial conception:* Casa Editrice Bonechi
*Publication Manager:* Monica Bonechi
*Picture research:* Alberto Andreini
*Graphic design and cover:* Maria Rosanna Malagrinò
*Video layout:* Alberto Douglas Scotti
*Text:* Panaghiótis Chrístou, Katharini Papastamatis
*Editing:* Simonetta Giorgi
*Translation:* Heather Mackay Roberts

© Copyright by CASA EDITRICE BONECHI, Via Cairoli, 18/b Firenze - Italia
Tel +39 -55 576841 - Fax +39 -55 5000766
E-mail: bonechi@bonechi.it    Internet: www.bonechi.it

*The photographs from the archives of* Casa Editrice Bonechi *are by*
Andrea Innocenti, Gianni Dagli Orti, Paolo Giambone, Studio Gabriel Koutoulias *and* Smara Ayacatsica.

*The photographs on pages 18, 20, 22, 29, 32, 33 bottom, 34/35, 41 top, 42 bottom, 49 top, 50, 61 bottom,
65, 76, 86, 108 bottom left are the property of* Gianni Dagli Orti.

*The photographs on pages 4/5, 8, 9, 10, 33 top, 37, 42 top, 46/47 bottom, 57, 74 right, 79, 85, 88, 90/91,
100, 101, 104, 108 bottom right, 111, 113, 114/115 are the property of* Scala.

*Drawings:* Alessandra Chiarlo *(pages 50, 58, 59, 60, 65, 78, 80, 88, 92, 96, 102, 120, 122)*;
Linda Imposimato *(pages 19, 38, 39, 45, 51, 67, 68, 69, 72, 73, 81, 89, 99, 116 )*.

*Printed in Italy by* Centro Stampa Editoriale Bonechi.

ISBN 88-8029-716-3

\* \* \*

# INTRODUCTION

*T*hroughout history man has felt the need to create myths and legends, to justify, explain and interpret his world. Since the beginning of time, no matter how sophisticated his society, he has tried to unravel the meaning of nature's mysteries and to understand the forces behind life: from atmospheric phenomena to the source of a spring, from the infinite variety and shades of flora to the destructive fury of an earthquake, even seeking to penetrate the hidden subtleties of the human psyche and spirit.

*The people of Greece, constantly enriched by the interchange and influx of a variety of cultures from the countries surrounding the Mediterranean, created a rich and detailed corpus of myths complete with clearly delineated genealogies, the logical development of ancient and widely narrated stories.*

*There is no definitive version of these myths. There are, on the contrary, often various ac-*

*counts of the same story, with divergencies and peculiarities related to their geographical origin. Variations in the same myth were obviously linked to the period and culture in which they gained popularity. Their development was also conditioned by their role in religious practice or as a metaphor for philosophical thought, or by the interreaction of myth and theatre.*

*Not only do these myths exist in often numerous versions but they have also become known to us in a variety of forms. Many are narrated in written sources (this work clearly offers only a limited selection from the numerous possible versions); we know of others from archaeology, with scenes depicted on vases, bronzes, reliefs, sarcophagi and on architectural decorative elements.*

*An additional difficulty is one of interpretation as these are stories many thousands of years old. The modern reader is faced not only with problems inherent in the narrative but more es-*

pecially with delving beyond the story into its symbolic meaning. We must further take into account violent or subtle shades of interpretation which already existed at the time of the myths' inception in Greece, Magna Grecia and Etruria, despite their relation in the same formal language.

It is also vital to remember that while the myths were being written and depicted in a variety of forms a lively oral tradition continued, shaping and changing them, adapting them to changing circumstances.

This eclecticism resulted in the formation of a corpus of myths which, despite diverse element, were adopted throughout the Greek world especially in those regions dominated by a supreme cultural centre: Athens extended her influence over Attica and the surrounding regions; Corinth over the north-eastern Peloponnese, and Sparta over Laconia and the southern Peloponnese.

The myths narrated here were shaped in those three regions. It should however be evident that this does not exclude the possibility that in more remote areas different versions developed which, in time, assumed greater importance than the original ones. Greek mythology should not be confused with Greek religion even though the two are inextricably linked, the myths forming the basis of religious beliefs, for a people with established practices and ceremonial rites, both public and private. In this lies the fundamental difference, for while the mythology was subject to change and development, religion was the immutable foundation.

Ancient Greek mythology has created universally recognised figures who have, over the generations, become models for behaviour and morality. The values and concepts represented by the mythological figures created in ancient Greece have been absorbed by all the cultures of the western world. The Greek myths were adopted by the Romans and interpreted by medieval scholars before the revival of interest occasioned by Humanism and the Renaissance. They were reinterpreted by the Neo-classical movement and Romanticism and endure in the metaphysical interpretations of modern art.

There is no country in the western world where the name of Ulysses fails to strike a particular chord; his cunning is proverbial, and we remember his yearning for his homeland; his name immortalised this century in James Joyce's masterpiece.

Who can forget the tragic story of Oedipus and his descendants in Thebes, and the "complex" named after him by Sigmund Freud? And what of the strength of Hercules, the fidelity of Penelope, Antigone's love for her brother, the mutual loyalty of Achilles and Patroclus, the beauty of Aphrodite, the power of Eros and the impartiality of Zeus?

*Zeus, father of the gods, enthroned and holding his sceptre, presides over all the gods on Mount Olympus. Central tondo in the ceiling of the Sala dell'Iliade. Fresco by Luigi Sabatelli (1772-1850). Florence, Pitti Palace.*

*Page 3: The chariot of Cybele, drawn by the proud lion, charging one of the giants rebelling against the gods of Olympus. This archaic scene reflects Man's atavistic fears which he sought both to exorcise and explain in mythical stories. Detail of the frieze on the north side of the Siphnian Treasury in the sanctuary of the Pythian Apollo. Delphi, Archaeological Museum (c. 525 B.C.).*

## CHAPTER I

# THE PRE-OLYMPIAN GODS

## Mother Earth and Uranus

Mother Earth (or Gaia) was born out of Chaos, the boundless emptiness of the Universe, and she was immediately followed by Eros, Love. Without any male intervention, Mother Earth, the primordial element from which the gods originated, gave birth to Pontus (the Sea) and Uranus (the Sky).

The union between Mother Earth and Uranus was extremely fruitful and among their progeny were the twelve Titans, six male and six female, and the Cyclops. The great size of Uranus meant that he alone could cover Mother Earth. She, however, tired of her excessive fertility and implored her sons to free her from the brutal embrace of Uranus. They all refused except her last-born, Cronos (Time), who, armed with a sickle, castrated his father and threw his testicles into the sea. The drops of blood falling from the mutilation of Uranus gave birth to the Erinnyes (Furies), the Giants and the Nymphs of the Ash-tree. The sickle thrown into the sea is traditionally identified with the island of Corfu, home of the Phaeacians, who sprung from the blood of Uranus.

*An impressive view of the Gulf of Corinth: the contrasting colours and the harmony of the natural elements evoke the mythical moment of creation when Gaia (the Earth) gave birth to Pontus (the Sea) and Uranus (the Sky).*

# CRONOS AND RHEA:
## THE BIRTH OF THE GODS

Cronos, after liberating Mother Earth and confining all his brothers to Tartarus (the lowest region of the earth, sited even below the Underworld), assumed power and married Rhea, one of his Titaness sisters.

Cronos had received a prophecy that he would be overthrown by one of his offspring, so he devoured each of them at birth: Hestia, Demeter, Hera, Hades and Poseidon. The maternal feeling of Rhea determined her salvation of her sixth child. To protect him from the brutal practice of his father, while expecting Zeus she took refuge in Crete, where at dead of night and in secret she gave birth in a cave on Mount Ida. To allay the suspicions of Cronos she gave him a large stone to eat, wrapped in a blanket.

Zeus grew rapidly, fed on the miraculous milk of the goat Amalthea, while Curetes and Corybantes (benevolent spirits), rattling their spears on their shields, concealed the cries of the child from the vengeance of Cronos.

# ZEUS AND THE TITANOMACHIA: THE OLYMPIAN PANTHEON

When he was fully grown, Zeus sought to overthrow his father. He asked advice of Metis (Prudence), who gave him an emetic potion to administer to Cronos so that he would regurgitate his devoured children. His liberated brothers then joined him in battle against Cronos who, in the meantime, had freed his own brothers from Tartarus. The ensuing ten year war (Titanomachia) resulted in the victory of Zeus and his brothers, the Olympian gods, while Cronos and the Titans were chased from the Sky and had to face merciless punishment by Zeus: the Titan Atlas, for example, was condemned to hold up the Sky for all eternity. After their victory the gods divided power among themselves by lot: Hades was given the Underworld and a helmet which made him invisible; Poseidon the control of the sea and a trident to shake the earth and waters; Zeus the heavens, the thunder and lightening, forged by the Cyclops, and he was also the predominant power in the Universe.

# THE BATTLE OF THE GIANTS: THE DEFINITIVE ESTABLISHMENT OF ORDER

The division of power did not ensure peace for very long, for when Mother Earth learnt that her sons the titans had once again been confined to the darkness of Tartarus she formed an alliance with others of her sons, the giants, born of the drops of blood shed by Uranus after his castration by Cronos.

The Olympian gods were then faced with the aggressive menace posed by the giants, enormous beings of terrifying appearance and overpowering strength, with bristling hair and serpent legs. All the Olympian gods joined in the battle but Zeus assumed the leadership with his powerful lightening and the protection of the aegis, the magical skin of the goat, Amalthea, who had nourished him. Athene, Zeus's favourite daughter, born to him directly out of his head, also fought under the protection of the aegis with the addition of the terrible Gorgon's head, given to her by Perseus as a sign of his gratitude for the help he had received from the goddess in the slaying of the Gorgon.

The Olympians had an exceptional ally in their battle against the giants in Heracles, a mortal who was welcomed by the gods in recognition of the strength and capability he had shown in performing a series of twelve arduous labours. His involvement led to the fulfilment of the prophecy that the defeat of the giants could only be brought about by the concerted attack from a god and a mortal.

# THE CREATION OF MAN

*The Titan Prometheus,
punished by Zeus for having
deceived him by helping man,
was imprisoned in the
mountains of the Caucasus
where the eagle of Zeus was
sent every day to devour his
liver. Opposite him stands the
Titan Atlas, forced to support
the weight of the heavens.
Laconian cup painted by the
Arcesilas Painter (c.550 B.C.).
Rome, Vatican Museums: inv.
n. 16592.*

Once the original Chaos was replaced by divine order, with the gods in the heavens and the brute forces confined to the Underworld, Zeus peopled the earth with a variety of beings and ordered his cousins, descended from the titans, Epimetheus and Prometheus, to distribute the gifts of the gods among these creatures.

Epimetheus began by distributing beauty to one species and strength to another, agility to those without strength, cunning to those without other defences, and intelligence to the physically weak.

His brother Prometheus (often considered the main benefactor of man and in some later traditions also his creator, having modelled him out of clay) intervened in this uneven distribution bestowing more gifts on human creation. Epimetheus had left man until last and finding he had run out of gifts condemned him to remain naked, weak and devoid of natural defences. Prometheus in his desire to assist mankind went so far as to deceive Zeus: during a solemn sacrifice he divided an ox, with the meat and innards covered by the skin in one part, and the bones concealed in the white fat in the other. Zeus, when asked to choose, before giving the second part to man, selected the white fat which concealed the bare bones and his anger towards humankind was so great that he withdrew one of their most precious gifts, fire.

Prometheus came once again to man's aid and having stolen several flames from the wheel of the Sun (or from the furnace of Hephaestus) he restored hope in the survival of the human race. Zeus then took his vengeance: Prometheus was fettered and chained to a mountain in the Caucasus, where the eagle of Zeus devoured his liver by day. Each night it regrew, only to be devoured again. He was only freed some thirty years later by Heracles who killed the ferocious eagle of Zeus. To Man Zeus sent Pandora, the first woman, modelled with the help of all the gods. As her name indicates ("she with all the gifts"), Pandora received beauty, grace, manual dexterity and persuasion, but spiteful Hermes also touched her heart with deceit and guile. Zeus sent her as a gift to Epimetheus who was won over by her great beauty and married her, forgetting the advice of his brother Prometheus, who had warned him to be very wary of the gifts bestowed by Zeus. No sooner had Pandora arrived on earth, and despite the warnings and strictures placed on her by Epimetheus, she was consumed with curiosity and opened the jar containing all wickedness which then spread throughout the world. Another tradition describes the vase as containing every kind of goodness which fled away when Pandora lifted the lid, which she replaced when Hope alone was left at the bottom.

Despite the gifts granted them by the gods and the help received from Prometheus as it progressed the human race failed to win favour with Zeus. He became so appalled by humanity's passions and vicious nature that he thought it best to destroy it by sending a universal flood. He decided to spare only one good and just couple: Deucalion, the son of Prometheus, and his wife Pyrrha, who as the daughter of Epimetheus was also his cousin. Warned by Zeus the couple built a wooden ark to shelter them from the flood waters which raged on the earth for nine days and nine nights. They eventually struck ground on the mountain peaks of Thessaly, from which the waters began to recede. They were welcomed by Hermes, sent by Zeus to grant them one unconditional wish: Deucalion and Pyrrha requested the company of other human creatures so as not to pass the rest of their lives in total solitude. Zeus then ordered them to throw the bones of their mother over their shoulders. The suggestion of such an impious act struck terror into the heart of Pyrrha, but Deucalion understood that stones were the bones of Mother Earth (Gaia). Tossing stones over their shoulders, Deucalion produced men and Pyrrha women, and so the earth was repopulated.

*Poseidon, Ares and Hermes in battle against the giants who are already succumbing to the superior strength of the gods. Attic red-figure pelike painted by an artist close to the Pronomos Painter (c. 400 B.C.). Athens, National Archaeological Museum: inv. no. 1333.*

# CHAPTER II

# THE GODS OF OLYMPUS

*Colossal head of Zeus. Part of an enormous marble statue of Zeus enthroned, discovered at Aegeira in Achaea. Generally identified with the work of the Athenian sculptor Eucleid, recorded at Aegeira in the 2nd century A.D. by Pausanius. Athens. National Archaeological Museum: inv. no.3377.*

## ZEUS, THE FATHER OF THE GODS

All sources are unanimous in citing Mount Olympus, on the border between Macedonia and Thessaly, as the dwelling place of the gods of the Greek Pantheon. On Olympus, the symbol *par excellence* of a celestial haven, the gods ruled in magnificent splendour, omnipotent on account of their divinity, but nevertheless subject to human passions and weaknesses, and often exhibiting a certain caprice in their dealings with each other and with man. The dramatic episodes accompanying their beginnings had a decisive effect on the slow unfolding of their complicated stories.

Zeus, born of Cronos and Rhea, nourished by the magical goat Amalthea, protected by Nymphs and Corybantes, and after his defeat of the Giants and Titans, the ruler with absolute power, held sway not only over mortals but reigned supreme over the other immortals, throned in the luminous heights of Olympus. As the god of light and of thunder and lightening he controlled all celestial manifestations and expressed his power through his attributes: lightening, a source of both illumination and destruction; the sceptre, a symbol of his regality; the eagle, his messenger; the aegis, the goat-skin of Amalthea, as impenetrable as armour. With these symbols to affirm his power, Zeus defended the established order, dispensed justice and protected regal power and the social hierarchy: all prerogatives which he exercised over men but also over the entire Pantheon.

From the union between Zeus and Hera, his wife and sister, were born Ares, the god of war, Ilithyia, the goddess of childbirth, capable of multiplying herself as the occasion demanded, and Hebe, the goddess of youth. Zeus's innumerable couplings with other females, both divine and human, gave birth to all the other gods, demi-gods and illustrious heroes of ancient Greece.

## THE TRANSFORMATIONS AND AMOROUS EXPLOITS OF ZEUS

The most important of Zeus's divine loves was undoubtedly Metis, the goddess of prudence, who was also the first of his wives. After several vain attempts to escape the advances of Zeus and her assumption of various disguises Metis was finally compelled to surrender to him and from their union Athene was conceived. Mother Earth had predicted that Metis would bear a daughter whose son would eventually overthrow Zeus and he therefore swallowed Metis to continue the gestation of their child himself.

In the meantime, Hera, jealous of Zeus's extra-marital exploits and of his ability to give birth without female participation, gave birth parthenogenetically to a son, Hephaestus, the god of fire. When the appointed time came it was this "half-brother" who split open the head of Zeus with his axe to allow Athene to emerge, already fully armed.

Equally celebrated is the union between Zeus and Leto, giving birth to Apollo, the god of light, and Artemis, the goddess of the hunt.

In this union, too, the jealous Hera intervened forcing Leto to wander the world in search of a place to give birth. Hera's prohibited every place whether on "terraferma or at sea" to give Leto shelter. The only spot to escape the prohibition was the island of Delos, in the centre of the Aegean, difficult to reach on account of strong underwater currents and therefore considered a floating island. It was here, neither at sea nor on terraferma that Leto gave birth to the most celebrated of the divine twins. As a sign of her gratitude Delos was secured to the seabed with four columns which have anchored it ever since and it became the most important of all the sanctuaries dedicated to Apollo.

Dione, the daughter of Uranus (or perhaps of Oceanus: tradition conflicts here) bore Zeus Aphrodite, the goddess of love. Dione is in fact the female form of the name Zeus and also signifies divinity of the luminous heavens. She was also the goddess of water and of the springs, where oracles were received, and was often associated with Oceanus, the father of all flowing waters and the personification of that element.

From his union with another of his sisters, Demeter, the goddess of corn and of cultivation, Zeus fathered Persephone (also known as Core, the maiden), future goddess of the underworld and companion to Hades.

Themis, goddess of justice and of eternal law, in addition to her role as the counsellor of Zeus (on her advice Zeus protected himself with the aegis, the skin of Amalthea, during his battle against the Giants) and of the other gods (she taught Apollo the art of divination), she also became espoused to the father of all the gods. In chronological order she was the second wife. They gave birth to numerous progeny, including the three Horae, the goddesses of the seasons (they only became associated with the hours

*The summit of Olympus. It was here, in the highest region of Thessaly, with its snowy peaks and deep ravines, below a brilliant blue sky, with the verdant pines and olives growing on the slopes, and the sea rolling in on the shores beneath, that the Greeks placed the celestial Pantheon, the mythical assembly of the gods, where they were entertained by the Graces and the Muses. On the orders of their father Zeus, named Olympic, the gods controlled the destiny of the men born to live and die on earth. Man's life was completely dominated and conditioned by the will of the gods. This was not always just, and often capricious, as the gods intervened in human affairs, sometimes to offer succour and sometimes to destroy, but never to be deeply touched by the lot of mankind as they always retained their Olympian detachment. The mountain was clearly a symbol, a symbol which became universal, of the unattainable serenity and imperturbability of the spirit, which became the objective of so many different philosophies.*

of the day in later traditions), and the three Moirae, the Fates that await us all (life, happiness, fortune, etc.) regulated according to an inflexible law which not even the gods could transgress: the three sisters regulated the length of every-man's life with a thread, spun by the first, wound by the second, and cut by the third at the final fatal hour.

Zeus coupled with Mnemosyne (Memory) in the pleasant region of Pierìa, in Thrace, for nine consecutive nights. A year later the young Titaness, the daughter of Uranus and Gaia, or Mother Earth, gave birth to nine daughters, the Muses. A celestial choir, their singing delighted their father Zeus and all the other gods. The Muses also personified various aspects of philosophy which established the primacy of music in the Universe: Calliope is the Muse of epic poetry, Clio of history, Polyhymnia of mime, Euterpe of the flute, Terpsichore of dance and of light poetry, Erato of choral music, Melpomene of tragedy, Thalia of comedy and Urania of astronomy.

The three Charites or Graces were born of the union between Zeus and Eurynome, whose upper body was in the shape of a woman but who had the form of a fish from the waist down. The Graces, who were originally associated with the life force in nature, and were only later seen as the personifications of Beauty, lived with the Muses on Mount Olympus and joined them in their entrancing song. Often depicted as three naked women, touching hand to shoul-

*Above: Ramnous (Attica). View of the ruins of the sanctuary, showing the temples dedicated to Nemesis, the goddess of divine vengeance, and to Themis, the goddess of justice.*
*Below: Leda and Zeus in the guise of a swan. The egg produced from this union gave birth to two sets of twins, including the beautiful Helen whose abduction by Paris gave rise to the Trojan War. Marble relief, 2nd century A.D.* Athens, National Archaeological Museum.

der, with the two outside figures facing the same direction and the middle Grace an opposite one, the three Graces traditionally hold direct influence over all work engaging the mind and artistic creation.

In his divine conquests Zeus relied on his manifest powers of persuasion and his considerable seductive charms, resorting to his claim to absolute authority in more difficult cases. His success with mortal women, who attracted him as much as the divinities, often necessitated the use of deception and metamorphosis.

His union with the Theban, Semele, the daughter of Cadmus and Harmonia, produced the god Dionysus, "born twice". Semele, like so many of Zeus's illicit loves, suffered harshly from Hera's jealousy. Hera, mindful of the promise Zeus had made to Semele to grant her anything her mortal heart desired, prompted her to ask Zeus to reveal himself to her in his full splendour. When Zeus appeared in his full power of lightening and thunderbolts Semele was destroyed but Zeus arranged for the protection of the tiny Dionysus. He was sewn into his thigh, hidden from Hera's vengeance, until the time came for his delivery.

Leda, descended from Deucalion, was the wife of Tyndareus, king of Sparta. Zeus became infatuated with her and in order to seduce her transformed himself into a white swan. The egg produced from their union gave birth to four children: Clytemnestra, later wife of Agamemnon and the mother of Orestes and Electra; Helen, who married Menelaus and whose infidelity occasioned the Trojan wars; and the two Dioscuri ("sons of Zeus"), Castor and Pollux or Polydeuces.

Another early tradition explains various elements in this myth. Zeus was infatuated by Nemesis, the goddess of divine vengeance, who to escape his embrace transformed herself into a variety of creatures until, while she was in the shape of a goose, Zeus had his will of her, transforming himself into a swan at Rhamnus, which then became the most important centre for the worship of the goddess. As the fruit of an undesired love the egg was abandoned by Nemesis and later found by some shepherds; they gave it to Leda who guarded it safely until the birth of the two sets of twins, whom she nurtured as her own. An identification of Leda with Nemesis is however extremely problematic given that the name is not of Greek origin but can be linked etymologically with the ancient Lycian word *lada*, or woman.

The king of Argos, Acrisius, heard a prophecy to the effect that he would be overthrown and killed by a son born to his daughter Danae. Attempting to escape his destiny Acrisius imprisoned Danae in an inaccessible bronze chamber, underground, where nevertheless she was visited by amorous Zeus in a shower of gold. The cries of Danae's baby Perseus revealed his birth to Acrisius, who then shut both mother and child in a wooden chest and cast them out to sea. They were washed ashore on the island of Seriphos.

Alcmene, the wife of Amphitryon, king of Tirynthus, sprang from the noble line of Perseus.

Overcome with desire for the beautiful queen, Zeus took advantage of the first union between Alcmene and her husband Amphitryon (long postponed on account of a vendetta) to take on the appearance of her husband so that in the same night Alcmene conceived Her-

*Zeus, disguised as a bull, captured Europa, the young daughter of King Phoenix, and carried her away across the seas. The myth became widely diffused quite early and was known to the Etruscans as is evident on this black-figure hydria, probably produced in Cerveteri (ancient Agylla) in about 530 B.C.*
*Rome, National Etruscan Museum, Villa Giulia.*

acles (fathered by Zeus) and Iphicles (fathered by Amphitryon): the divine origin of the one and the natural origin of the other were only revealed at their birth.

Europa, the beautiful daughter of Phoenix, king of rich Sidon (or perhaps of Tyre), was playing on the sand with her companions when she was spotted by Zeus, who, inflamed with passion, transformed himself into a white bull with horns like a crescent moon and lay down at the feet of Europa. Although frightened at first, Europa gradually lost her fear and climbed onto the bull's back whereupon the creature made swiftly for the waves, ignoring the maiden's piteous cries. She clung to his horns for fear of falling and was transported to Crete were Zeus lay with her under an enormous plane tree, beside a spring of fresh water, where Europa conceived Minos, Sarpedon and Rhadamanthus. The plane tree, the silent witness to this amorous act, was granted the privilege of never loosing its leaves.

The passionate Zeus was also susceptible to the charms of young boys, as we learn from the story of Ganymede, a youthful descendent of Dardanus, the first of the royal line of Troy. Ganymede, considered the most beautiful of all mortals, had just reached adolescence when, leading his father's flock to pasture in the mountains outside Troy, was approached by Zeus with the characteristic gifts of ephebic love (a cockerel and a wheel with a clasp). Zeus stole him away to Mount Olympus where he received the gift of eternal youth and became cup-bearer to the father of the gods.

*Facing page: Ganymede, the young Trojan prince, considered the most beautiful of all mortals, was stolen by Zeus after the father of the gods had presented him with a cockerel and a wheel. Detail, red-figure Attic krater, painted by the Berlin Painter (c. 500 B.C.). Paris, Louvre: inv. no. G 175.*

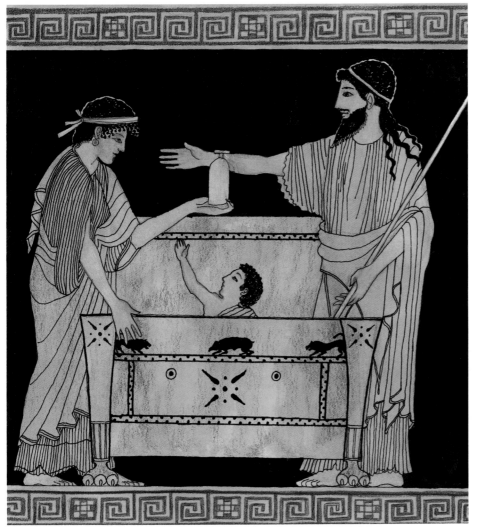

*Danae and Perseus as a child land on Seriphos to emerge safe and sound from the chest in which they had been imprisoned by Acrisius. They are welcomed on the island by King Polydectus. Drawing after a red-figure hydria painted by the Painter of Danae (c. 440 B.C.). Boston, Museum of Fine Arts: inv. no. 13200.*

# HERA, THE MOTHER OF THE GODS

The most important of the Olympian goddesses, the daughter of Cronos and Rhea, and therefore both sister and wife to Zeus, Hera was the protectress of the female world and as the legitimate wife of the father of all the gods was also the guardian of wives and of matrimony. According to tradition the love between Zeus and Hera existed long before their marriage but they were obliged to meet in secret before the sumptuous nuptial celebrations.

Angered by the habitual infidelities of her husband Hera was jealous and vindictive not only in dealing with her rivals but also with regard to their progeny whom she delighted in persecuting. Heracles for example underwent endless suffering on account of her anger, as it was she who was responsible for the challenge of the twelve labours. Semele suffered a violent and tragic end, and Leto too was persecuted by the goddess.

Zeus's numerous infidelities were not the only cause of friction between the couple, as is evident from their dispute with Teiresias, which cost him his sight. When asked whether the male or female drew greater pleasure from the sexual act, Teiresias, whom Zeus had granted the privilege of enjoying the experience of both partners, answered that on a scale of one to ten, the man's pleasure could be measured as one while the woman's measured nine. The infuriated Hera blinded him, although Zeus rewarded him with the gift of foresight.

# ATHENE, THE STRENGTH OF WISDOM

The goddess, delivered fully grown and fully armed from the head of Zeus, was immediately recognised as his alter ego, and was presented by her father with the aegis from Amalthea. Athene is the goddess of wisdom rather than of war, the domain of her brother Ares. She did however play a decisive role in the battle against the giants, when for example she immobilised the Giant Enceladus by hurling against him the whole island of Sicily. She also intervened strategically in the Trojan wars giving her support to a number of the heroes including Achilles and Odysseus. She guided Perseus with intelligence and stealth to the discovery of those secrets which enabled him to decapitate the Gorgon and she gave constant protection to her favourite hero Heracles while he was engaged on the twelve long labours.

Poseidon and Athene put forward rival claims to the possession of Athens and Attica. All the gods judged the contest, the prize being the bestowal of the victor's name on the city. Victory was destined to the one the gods considered had offered the city the greater gift. Poseidon struck the rock of the Acropolis in Athens with his trident bringing forth a stream of salty water whereas Athene stamped her foot and gave rise to the first olive tree in history. She naturally was victorious, the city took her name, and the olive became sacred to her, a symbol of peace and prosperity.

*Above: view of Argos; a famous sanctuary dedicated to Hera stood near the city. Below: Athene, goddess of wisdom. Bronze statue (c. 375 B.C.) from Piraeus, the port of Athens. Piraeus, Archaeological Museum.*

*Athene, with Victory in hand and the shield hiding the figure of Erichthonius. When Hephaestus tried to violate Athene she resisted his advances but was smeared with his seed, which she immediately wiped clean with a cloth. The cloth, thrown to the ground, gave birth to the serpent-son Erichthonius. Athene of Varvakion (2nd century B.C.); copy of the Parthenos Athene carved by Phydias between 440 and 430 B.C. for the Parthenon. Athens, National Archaeological Museum: inv. no.129.*

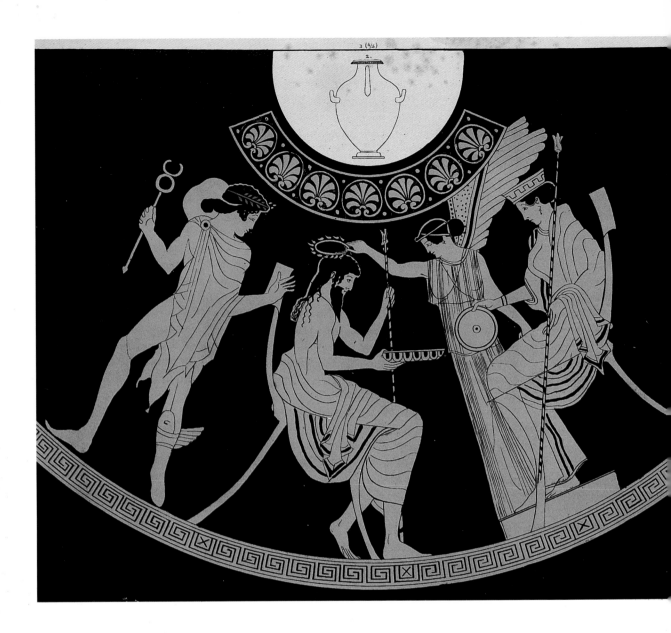

# HEPHAESTUS, THE POWER TO FORGE METALS

*The most famous hierogamy of classical antiquity, the divine marriage between Zeus and Hera, the couple which dominated the Greek Pantheon. The father of the gods is crowned by Victory, assisted by Mercury who is ready to take flight to communicate orders from Zeus. Drawing after a red-figure Attic hydria, painted c. 440 B.C. Leiden Museum.*

The parthenogenetic son of Hera, who was jealous of Zeus's ability to gestate and then produce Athene from his own head, Hephaestus is the blacksmith-god, with matchless skill in the working of metals. Born weak and lame, he was thrown by his disgusted mother down from the heights of Olympus, and fell for a whole day before landing on the island of Lemnos, where he set up his forge under a volcano. To revenge his cruel rejection by his mother he made her a magic throne which kept Hera prisoner. The pleas of the gods to persuade Hephaestus to return to Olympus to free his mother were all in vain and it was only Dionysus who, having made Hephaestus drunk on wine, brought him back to Olympus straddled over the back of a mule. In compensation Hephaestus was given the beautiful Aphrodite as his wife while Dionysus was rewarded for his pains by becoming one of the Olympian Pantheon.

# POSEIDON, POWER OVER THE SEAS

Poseidon, together with Zeus and Hera, is one of the most important of the gods, and one of the oldest. He has dominion over the seas which he can agitate at will by striking his trident, causing violent repercussions and earthquakes. He is generally depicted steering his chariot, drawn by dolphins or fabulous sea-creatures, swiftly through the waves which rise around but never touch him.

He had numerous progeny, almost as many as Zeus, but in contrast to his brother, who generated benevolent offspring the children of Poseidon are celebrated for their malevolence. His union with the Gorgon gave birth to Chrysaor and the winged horse, Pegasus, while Toosa bore him the Cyclops Polyphemus, later blinded by Odysseus, who was then punished for the rest of his voyage home.

*Poseidon, the god of the sea is shown poised to throw his trident, now lost. Bronze statue known as the Poseidon, of Cape Artemision, discovered off the island of Eubea and attributed to Calamides (c. 460 B.C.) Athens, National Archaeological Museum: inv. no.I5161.*

## DEMETER, THE GODDESS OF PLENTY

In contrast to Gaia, Mother Earth, who is revered as a cosmic element and the genitrix of all things, Demeter is the goddess of cultivation and therefore of fruit and above all of corn which plays a fundamental role in her story and especially in the fate of her daughter Persephone (Core), fathered by Zeus. Persephone had a carefree upbringing in the company of her sisters, also daughters of Zeus, Athene and Artemis, until her uncle, Hades, the brother of Zeus who reigned in the Underworld, became enraptured with her. Zeus, who did not want to commit his daughter to eternal reclusion in the darkness of the Underworld, denied Hades the hand of Persephone.

Hades then stole her from a field where she was picking flowers near the entrance to the Underworld in the region of Eleusis (other versions suggest she was taken from the plain of Enna at the foot of Mount Etna in Sicily).

*Eleusis, sanctuary of Demeter and Persephone: detail of the grotto of Hades, known as Ploutonion, and thought to be the entrance to the Underworld. It was through this opening that Pluto, or Hades, stole the maiden Persephone to carry her into the Underworld as his bride.*

In desperation at the sudden and mysterious disappearance of her daughter, whose raptor was unknown as his head had been veiled by the shades of night, Demeter refused to return to Olympus but began to wander the world in search of Persephone, a search that lasted nine days and nine nights. During this time she neither ate nor drank, nor did she wash or attend to her appearance in any way, but followed the light of the two flaming torches she carried. On her travels Demeter, who now appeared an old woman, came to Eleusis where she sat down on a stone which from that time since has been called *aghélastos petra*, "the stone without joy", in memory of her suffering. Demeter then visited the court of the king of Eleusis, Celeus, where she found

*Eleusis, detail of the sanctuary of Demeter and Persephone, built on the spot where Demeter lay down to rest in a state of exhaustion after the long search for her daughter, who had been stolen by Hades.*

refuge and refreshment and even one of her old servants, Iambe, who coaxed smiles from the goddess with her playful stories. In recognition of her kind treatment Demeter revealed the secrets of cultivation of corn to Triptolemus, the youngest of Celeus's sons, and charged him to spread his knowledge throughout the world. The most important of all the sanctuaries to Demeter and Persephone grew up at Eleusis, around the sacred stone where the goddess had rested. Her cult was founded on the mysteries surrounding cultivation, revealed only to the initiated. Demeter's voluntary exile from Olympus left the earth sterile and the natural order, reflected in the rotation of the seasons, in total confusion. Zeus intervened and ordered his brother Hades to restore Persephone to her mother. This, however, was no longer possible, as Persephone had inadvertently eaten a seed from the pomegranate in violation of the decree that those seeking return to the earth must abstain from any sustenance. Zeus then proposed a cunning compromise allowing Hades to keep Persephone for only part of the year while her mother then had her for the rest. Demeter, satisfied, returned to Mount Olympus and the natural order of the seasons was re-established. And so, every year Persephone is released from the Underworld and the buds of spring burst free having remained hidden in the earth, made sterile by Demeter during the cold of winter, when Persephone stays with Hades.

*Hermes with the young Dionysus in his arms. Marble statue discovered in the temple to Hera at Olympia, probably an original work by the great Athenian sculptor, Praxitiles (circa 340 B.C.). Olympia, Archaeological Museum.*

# HERMES, THE MESSENGER OF THE GODS

T he messenger of the Olympian gods, Hermes is also the god of shepherds and is frequently depicted as *Chriophorus*, or with a lamb over his shoulder. He is also the god of cunning and shrewdness, of barter and therefore of commerce as well as of theft.

Hermes was born to the nymph Maia in a cave on Mount Cyllene in Arcadia having been fathered by Zeus at dead of night while all the other gods and mortals slept. He was born on the fourth day of the month, consecrated to him ever since (in the Roman world he was called Mercury, and hence the French and Italian names for Wednesday: *Mercredi* and *Mercoledì*).

Shortly after his birth when still in swaddling bands lying in his cradle he showed amazing precocity: he wriggled free of his bands and ran to far off Thessaly where his brother Apollo was grazing his cows.

*Hermes, as the divine messenger, was also obliged to accompany the spirits of the dead to the world beyond, the confines of which were guarded by two fierce sphinxes who prevented any contact between the world of the living and the dead. Attic black-figure oinochoe (c. 560 B.C.). Athens, National Archaeological Museum: inv. no. 19159.*

Hermes stole several head of cattle and led them back to Greece where he hid them in a grotto close to the city of Pylos, having concealed their tracks. He then returned to his mother's cave on Mount Cyllene but before wrapping himself again in his swaddling bands he killed a tortoise, hollowed out its shell and strung it with the intestines of some of the cattle stolen from Apollo, to make the first lyre. Apollo, when he realised he had been robbed, remonstrated with Maia but she, seeing Hermes swaddled in the cradle as she had left him, would not accept his guilt. Zeus intervened and demanded that Hermes return the cattle, but Apollo enchanted by the sound of the newly invented lyre, accepted it in exchange for his animals and became a master of the instrument. Later Hermes, watching over the cattle he had bartered from Apollo, also invented a pipe, cut from reeds, and once again Apollo coveted it and gave him his golden wand, or caduceus, in exchange; it became the symbol of Hermes in his role as messenger of the gods and therefore of all ambassadors.

# APHRODITE, BEAUTY AND LOVE

The daughter of Zeus and Dione, or according to another tradition of Uranus (sprung from his testicles, when they were severed and thrown into the sea by Cronos), Aphrodite is the goddess of love and of beauty and although married to Hephaestus, the lame Smith-god, her great love was for Ares. Her amorous adventures are celebrated, and provoked the wrath and vengeance of Hephaestus. On one occasion he caught Aphrodite and Ares in bed together in an enormous fishing net he had made of metal and from which there was no possible escape. He then summoned all the gods to laugh at the lovers' predicament. From the union of Aphrodite and Ares sprang Eros and Anteros (Love and literally "Against Love" but meaning "Mutual Love"), Deimos and Phobos (Terror and Fear), Harmonia, future wife of the king of Thebes, Cadmos, and lastly Priapus, the god of gardens.

Aphrodite also chose lovers from among the mortals, the most significant being Anchises, king of Troy. Their union gave birth to Aeneas, the founder of Rome, and it was his immortal origin which gave rise to the flourishing cult of his mother in Rome where she was worshipped as Venus.

Aphrodite intervened in the Trojan war, certainly more than might reasonably have been justified by her love for Anchises, and to some extent it was her own beauty which caused the outbreak of hostilities. It was on the day of the wedding between Peleus and Thetis, the parents of the great Achilles, that Eris (Discord) threw an apple destined for the most beautiful of the three goddesses, Hera, Athene and Aphrodite. Zeus suggested that Paris, the young prince of Troy, should decide the contest. Brought into his presence at Troade, each goddess proclaimed her superior beauty and promised Paris the most beguiling gifts if chosen. Hera promised him sovereignty over all Asia, and Athene invincibility in war, but neither of these gifts was as attractive to Paris as the hand of Helen, the most beautiful woman on earth, promised to him by Aphrodite. And so Aphrodite won the contest and Helen was instrumental in causing the most celebrated of wars. Aphrodite always gave her support to Troy in the long years of fighting, and her protection of Anchises, Aeneas and his son Ascanius (also known as Iulus), prevented the extermination of the royal line.

*The goddess Aphrodite, modestly covers her beauty as she steps from the water. Marble Roman copy of Greek original (1st century B.C.). Athens, National Archaeological Museum.*

*The goddess of beauty is born from a shell and emerges from the white foam of the waves. Terracotta votive statue of the 4th century B.C. Athens, National Archaeological Museum.*

# ARES, THE GOD OF WAR

Ares, the son of Hera and Zeus, is the god of war and all martial activities. He intervenes not only in heroic-mythological enterprises but also directly in wars and is depicted in literary sources as enjoying carnage and slaughter. He intervened in the Trojan war at random, first giving aid to the Trojans and then to the Greeks, his intervention governed by little more than caprice. Many of the adventures engaging his attention took place in Thrace, a wild area in the north of Greece inhabited by his daughters, the Amazons, born of his union with the nymph Harmonia. Although he often took a leading role in conflicts he was rarely victorious. More often he withdrew in disgrace from the exchange, as when he deserted Hector in his conflict with Diomedes, or when he withdrew from the feuding gods under the walls of Troy. On both these occasions he took refuge on Mount Olympus because Athene had made his position untenable. At other times his brutal fury was unfavourably set against the calculated cunning of Heracles, as in the fatal encounter between Heracles and Ares's son Cycnus.

*The battle between the gods and the giants. The divine twins Apollo and Artemis fight against Cantarus, Ephialtes and Ipertes. Detail of the frieze on the north side of the Siphnian Treasury, a votive building with sculpture decoration dedicated by the inhabitants of the island of Siphnos in the sanctuary of the Pythian Apollo (c. 525 B.C.). Delphi, Archaeological Museum.*

# APOLLO, LIGHT AND PURITY

Apollo, with his arm raised, declares victory in favour of the Lapiths in their struggle against the Centaurs. Detail of the west pediment from the Temple of Zeus at Olympia (c. 460 B.C.). Olympia, Archaeological Museum.

A god, radiant in benevolent light, the Sun rose from the shades of night (Leto means "the hidden one"). Apollo symbolises the triumph of day over the dark power of night and therefore all the positive effects of light and sunshine. He was venerated as Targelion, referring to the fertile warmth that ripens fruit (the name Targelion indicating May); as Smintheus (from *sminthos,* rat); and as Parnopius (from *parnops,* grasshopper). He was worshipped as the destroyer of rats and locusts, and as

man's liberator from the pestilences these creatures carry. He is also the divine inspiration of lyrical beauty, and therefore of music and poetry, and directs the choir of the Muses, the daughters of Zeus and Mnemosyne. His symbols are a bow and arrows, emblematic of the power of the sun's rays; his head is crowned with laurel and he plays a cithara with a plectrum, appropriate attributes of the god of music.

The swan, the wolf, and the dolphin are sacred to him: the swan because at the time of his birth, the seventh day of the month, a flock of swans circled the island of Delos, where his mother had her lying-in seven times; the wolf, who causes such terror in the winter, because Apollo puts him to flight (Apollo is frequently referred to as Lycius, from *lykos,* wolf); the dolphin because it was much beloved of Apollo and he often assumed its form, to cross the waves swiftly, and not infrequently to save the shipwrecked.

The most famous of his attributes is however the tripod, alluding to his powers of divination which he could confer on the priestesses in his sanctuaries. Apollo had visited Delphi, in Phocides, and killed the dragon, Python, charged with the protection of the oracle of Themis, the goddess of law, beside the chasm emitting trance-inducing emanations and the power of prophecy. The dragon had carried out widespread devastation in the region, destroying crops, killing peasants, sacking villages and polluting springs and streams. After Apollo had slaughtered Python and taken possession of the oracle, he became known as Apollo Pythonus and dedicated a bronze tripod to the sanctuary and conferred divinatory powers on one of the priestesses; he took her into his service, and she has been called the Pythoness ever since. Seated on Apollo's tripod the priestess inhaled the vapours from the chasm and chewed laurel leaves, giving Sibylline responses to the questions addressed to her which were then unravelled by those charged with the interpretation of her meaning.

As the god of beauty, with fine physical traits in addition to his moral attributes, Apollo is held to be the most attractive of the gods; tall with a fine head of hair, he was involved in numerous amorous adventures with mortals and goddesses alike.

Eros, the young god of love, irritated by Apollo's singing and annoyed by his mockery of his first attempts with the bow and arrow (with which, in truth, he showed great skill) determined to have his revenge. He therefore provoked Apollo's infatuation with Daphne, the beautiful daughter of the river god Peneus in Thessaly. Daphne fled from Apollo into the mountains where he pursued her and was about to reach her when Peneus, in answer to his daughter's prayers, transformed her into a laurel tree *(dafne* in Greek), which from then on became a tree sacred to Apollo.

He loved to dally with the Nymphs and one of these, Cyrene, bore him Aristaeus, the demi-god who taught men dairy skills, bee-keeping and wine cultivation, as well as the use of nets and traps in hunting.

His most famous love among the mortals was for Hecuba, the wife of Priam, king of Troy, who gave birth to Troilius, the youngest prince of the royal line. According to an oracle, as long as Troilius lived to be twenty Troy could not be defeated. And so it was that Achilles hid in ambush for Troilius, who had crept secretly from the city with his sister Polyxena to visit a spring: he to water the horses, she to collect water in a vase.

His union with Coronis, daughter of the king of the Lapiths, led to the birth of Asclepius, the god of medicine.

*Apollo flying on a swan, one of his sacred animals, to the land of the Hyperboreans. Fragment, red-figure plate painted by the great Athenian painter Euphronius (c. 510 B.C.) and dedicated as an ex-voto, from the Acropolis. Athens, National Archaeological Museum: inv. 19274.*

Apollo also loved Troilius's sister, Cassandra, the daughter of Hecuba and Priam, whom he seduced with a promise to reveal to her the art of prophecy. Cassandra, having been instructed, rejected Apollo, who punished her by declaring that her prophecies would never gain credence.

Apollo also fell in love with those of his own sex, notably Hyacinth and Cyparissus, who transformed into a flower and a tree, stand as reminders of the god's close association with the natural world.

Hyacinth was a young Spartan prince whose extraordinary beauty inflamed the passions of Apollo. While they were throwing the discus together one day, Zephyr, the god of the west wind, also violently attracted to Hyacinth and jealous of Apollo, blew the discus off course to dash against Hyacinth's skull. Apollo was grief-stricken, and to immortalise his love a flower grew from the blood were he lay dead: the hyacinth, on which the lover's initials are still to be traced.

Cyparissus, a handsome young descendent of Heracles, was given one of Apollo's sacred deer as a token of his love. The tame animal became the faithful companion of Cyparissus but one summer's day while the deer lay sleeping in the shade of some bushes Cyparissus slew it by mistake with his javelin. In desperation he wanted only to die and asked Apollo that his tears might fall for all eternity. The god transformed him into a tree, the cypress, the symbol of sorrow with its tears always in evidence (either the cypress's small cones or the sap often visible on its trunk).

*Apollo in combat with Heracles for possession of the sacred and prophetic tripod which stood in his sanctuary at Delphi. Red-figure amphora painted c. 510 B.C. by the Athenian painter, Phintias.* Tarquinia, National Archaeological Museum.

# ARTEMIS, THE VIRGIN HUNTRESS

A rtemis, Apollo's twin sister, was born just before her brother and was therefore able to assist her mother, Leto, at his birth on the island of Delos. She chose the eternal youth offered to virgins and dedicated her life exclusively to the hunt. Armed with her bow and arrows, the goddess was held responsible for sudden and painless deaths and for women who died in childbirth.
Both volatile and vindictive, she was relentless in her punishment

of those who offended her. Oineus, for example, having failed to perform a sacrifice in her honour was pursued by the terrible Calydonian wild-boar. Orion, the giant hunter son of Poseidon, who tried to violate her, was stung by one of her scorpions on the heel and killed: both scorpion and victim were transformed into constellations, with Orion always appearing to take flight from Scorpio: Actaeon, the son of Aritaeus, who chanced to spy her while she bathed naked with her nymphs, was transformed into a deer and chased by his own pack of fifty hounds and torn to pieces. The hounds then searched vainly through the forest, baying for their lost master, until the centaur Chiron took pity on them and modelled a statue in the image of Actaeon. Artemis was no less cruel with her own followers. When Callisto, the virgin huntress, was seduced by Zeus, who had disguised himself as Artemis (Callisto would let no man near her) and her shame was revealed while bathing (she gave birth to Arcas, the ancestor of the Arcadians), Artemis changed her into a bear and sent her pack in pursuit, but Zeus took pity on Callisto and raised her to heaven, transformed into the constellation of the Great Bear.

*Artemis, the goddess of the hunt and Apollo's divine twin, born of Zeus and Latona (and always opposed by Hera, the legitimate wife of Zeus). Bronze statue discovered at Piraeus, the port of Athens. Greek original of the mid-4th century B.C. (Presumably she held a bow in her left hand). Piraeus, Archaeological Museum.*

*Actaeon surprises Artemis bathing: the goddess wrecked terrible vengeance on the young hunter for his mistake. Ceiling fresco by Giovanni Francesco Romanelli (1610-1662). Paris, Louvre.*

*Dionysus, the god of wine. Head of a marble statue of the 3rd century B.C. from the sanctuary dedicated to him on the island of Thasos. Thasos, Archaeological Museum.*

# DIONYSUS,
## THE GOD OF WINE

One of the most important of the second generation of gods, Dionysus, known to the Romans as Bacchus, is the god of wine and of viticulture, but also personifies natural energy bringing fruit to maturation on the plant together with the beneficial effects of water. The association of the god with water occurs throughout his story: tradition relates how Dionysus ("born twice") was born directly from Zeus having been sewn into his thigh after the death of his mother Semele. The mortal Semele was burnt to death when, at the suggestion of the jealous Hera, she asked to see her divine lover in his full splendour. After his birth Dionysus was entrusted to Hermes who delivered him to the Nymphs, to be brought up on Mount Nissa. An obvious interpretation of the myth is as follows: Semele is the earth scorched by the violent rays of the summer sun, but the fruit of her womb, the life-giving warmth which leads to maturity is saved and sustained by the Water Nymphs, the clouds providing rain.

*Dionysus and Ariadne. The god, naked and in a sensual pose, expressive of the voluptuous abandon induced by drinking wine, gently lays his leg over his lover, Ariadne's, thigh. Dionysus' infatuation with the princess saved her from the sad fate of her abandonment by Theseus on the island of Naxos. Detail of a krater, with two handles in gilt bronze of c. 340 B.C. from the tomb chamber discovered at Derveni in Macedonia.* Saloniki, Archaeological Museum.

Dionysus was then raised in the wild woods and sustained by nature before planting vines and becoming drunk on the sweet juice of the grape. Crowned with vine-leaves and ivy, he travels the world in his chariot drawn by panthers, traditionally followed by a band of satyrs, men with tails, goat's hooves and large animal ears, and Maenads, women engaged in frantic dances, overcome with the ecstasy provoked by their proximity to Dionysus.

Dionysus then taught men the art of cultivation and of viticulture, he founded new cities and instituted cults in his name wherever he travelled. He introduced a new approach to life making it more joyous and sociable. It was on one of his many voyages, when travelling to the island of Naxos, that Dionysus, disguised as a boy with thick curly hair and a purple cloak, was approached by a vessel belonging to some Tyrrenian pirates. Unaware of his true identity the pirates captured the god and then headed east intent on selling him as a slave. Dionysus in an instant revealed all the power of his divinity: he immobilised the ship with garlands of vines, he transformed the oars into serpents while the boarding planks sprouted ivy tendrils, and lions and panthers appeared from nowhere. The terrified pirates abandoned ship but as they dived into the sea were transformed into dolphins. Continuing his voyage to Naxos Dionysus found Ariadne abandoned there by Theseus and returned with her to Olympus, having completed his mission of educating men in cultivation and having established his cult throughout the world.

Worshipped as the great benefactor of humanity and for having enriched civilisation, (qualities he shared with other benevolent deities like Apollo and Demeter) Dionysus, through the magical effects of his wine, lifted man's spirits, encouraged song and inspired poetry while alleviating the cares and sufferings of the body and the mind. But while his cult in moderation (or rather the moderate use of wine) might have a beneficial effect, Dionysus is also capable of deranging the human mind with his potent ecstasies, as is apparent in the stories of Lycurgus and Pentheus. Lycurgus, king of Thrace, refused to give Dionysus, when still a child, a cordial reception as he passed through his lands with his loud and unruly band of followers, and was anxious to prevent the establishment of the cult in Thrace.

A Maenad, in a Dionysian ecstacy, holds the tirsos (the sacred branch crowned with a pinecone and wrapped in ivy) in one hand and a situla ( a small bucket) full of wine, in the other. She moves to the rhythmical and repetitive music of the double flute, the typical accompaniment to Dionysian revels. Detail of a drawing on a red-figure krater of Siculian, or early Sicilian, production (c. 340 B.C.) Lipari, Archaeological Museum. The Maenads, or Bacchantes, who in the potent state of ecstasy induced by Dionysus's wine, tore to pieces the young animals to be sacrificed to their god. They, together with the satyrs, or Silenes, who were sexually aroused by the dancing Maenads, and Pan, were the permanent followers in Dionysus's band.

He even tried to arrest the god, who took refuge at sea with the Nereid Thetis (the mother of the great Achilles), so driving Lycurgus to imprison the Bacchantes, Dionysus's rowdy followers. In revenge the god freed the Bacchantes of their fetters and drove Lycurgus to madness. The king, suffering severe hallucinations, took an axe and struck down his son, then cut off his extremities, and injured his own leg, all in the belief that he was cutting down ivy, a plant sacred to Dionysus. Lycurgus, recovering his sanity, realised the extent of his personal loss but also the afflictions he had brought on his people by opposing Dionysus, for the whole land had been made barren. The oracles declared that the barrenness would continue unless Lycurgus were put to death and so he was, by his own people, tied to four wild horses and torn to pieces.

Pentheus, king of Thebes, tried to prevent the Theban women from joining in Dionysian revels, despite the repeated warnings from the soothsayer Teiresias. Pentheus tried to chain Dionysus and scorned his power even though the god dissolved the chains intended to fetter him and destroyed the royal palace with flames. Pentheus then concealed himself in a hollow tree on Mount Cithaeron to observe the Theban women in their Dionysian revels, which no outsider might witness. The women, inflamed with the ecstasy of the rites and transformed into Bacchantes, spied their king and in their frenzy took him for an animal which they then sacrificed to Dionysus, tearing him from limb to limb.

His own mother Agave tore off his head, and believing it to be that of a lion impaled it on a branch and carried it in triumph to Thebes. After the ceremony, Agave and the other women, mindful of what had occurred, recognised the overwhelming power of Dionysus who had chosen so to punish such sacrilege. Agave, in remorse, fled from Thebes.

*The death of Pentheus, king of Thebes, torn to pieces by the Maenads (two, dressed in leopard skins, hold his torso with the fresh viscera hanging beneath, one holds his clothes, while another raises his detached leg) while a satyr withdraws horrified, making a leap backwards. Drawing after a red-figure vase painted by the Athenian Douris (c. 480 B.C.). On the other side of the vase more Maenads, holding Pentheus's dismembered body, dance before the seated Dionysus, to the music of the double flute, played by a satyr.* Toronto E.Borowski Collection.

# HESTIA, THE GODDESS OF THE HEARTH

T he sister of Zeus and Hera, the Vesta of the Romans, Hestia is the goddess of the domestic hearth and its personification as the centre of all family life. While all the other gods and goddesses left Mount Olympus to travel throughout the world she never left it: as the hearth was the religious centre of the house, Hestia was the religious heart of the celestial dwelling-place.
Fire was instrumental in family religious sacrifices and so the image of the great protective divinity always appeared beside the hearth. Hestia also represented the temple of domestic religion and had a role of fundamental importance in all the sacrifices and religious ceremonies celebrated in the family. As every house was therefore a temple in her honour there were no sacred buildings dedicated to her but she was a focus of worship in Greece in every temple, whatsoever its dedication. No sacrifice took place without a libation to Hestia at its beginning and its end. She was involved in every ceremonial feast with the privilege of being nominated before all others and was always offered the first fruits of any sacrifice.
As fire is the symbol of purity so the goddess was conceived as both chaste and pure and chose to remain so. The repeated offers of marriage from both Apollo and Poseidon met with her firm refusal and her unshaken resolve to remain an eternal virgin. Her priestesses too were expected to lead chaste lives.
The cult of Hestia in the temple of Apollo at Delphi, with its fire permanently lit, became the symbol of national unity recognised by all the people of Greece.

*Above: Hestia, goddess of the hearth in both divine and human dwellings, sits with her head covered on a precious fur-covered stool with lion paws feet, in the company of the gods on Mount Olympus. Drawing after a red-figure Attic vase made by the potter Sosias, and painted by the Sosias Painter, c. 500 B.C. Berlin-Charlottenburg, Antikenmuseum: inv. no. F 2278.*
*Below: view of the temple of Apollo at Delphi.*

# ASCLEPIUS, THE GOD OF MEDICINE

Many conflicting stories surround the birth of Asclepius, the god of medicine, some referring to him as the son of Apollo and Coronis ("crow" in Greek), the daughter of Phlegyas, the Thessalian king of the Lapiths, while others say he was born of Apollo and Arsinoe, the daughter of Leucippus, king of Messenia. But the story relating to Coronis is most frequently cited: Apollo fell in love with her and Asclepius was the fruit of their union. Coronis was unfaithful to Apollo however and he was informed of her meeting with her mortal lover by a crow (or by his own power of divination). In revenge he killed her but rescued his unborn child from Coronis as she lay on the funeral pyre. The baby was entrusted to the good centaur Chiron who taught him the art of medicine in which Asclepius soon excelled. He discovered how to resuscitate the dead with the blood of the Gorgon which he had received from

Athene. This practice earned him the envy of Zeus who, in the light of the numerous resurrections enacted by Asclepius, feared an overthrow of the cosmic order and killed Asclepius with a thunderbolt. Apollo then avenged his son's death by killing the Cyclops, who made lightening for Zeus, and withdrawing from Olympus. After his death Asclepius appeared as a constellation, and his medicinal power was symbolised by snakes coiled about a staff.

Asclepius is a benevolent god, offering physical well-being, protection from illness and the resuscitation of the dead. He was an object of veneration in many parts of Greece, with important centres at Epidaurus in Argolides, Sicyon, Athens, Pergamus, and Smyrna and later in Rome on Tiber Island (now the site of a modern hospital). Every sanctuary was flanked by a hospital in which pilgrims and patients gathered. They were treated with ointments, balms and tissanes as well as surgical interventions but mainly with the recitation of magic incantations and *incubation:* prayers and sacrifices inducing the patient to sleep when Asclepius would then appear in a dream to suggest the remedy for the patient's ills.

The medical tradition founded by Asclepius was continued by his followers, the Asclepiades.

Asclepius had children by Epione, "the one who soothes", two of whom (Podalirus and Machaon) are mentioned by Homer. Among the others are Hygiea (health), often depicted together with her father, Iase, Panacea, Aglaea, and Aceso all names reminiscent of the medicinal and salutary powers of their father.

*Hygiea, goddess of health and the daughter of Asclepius from whom she inherited the attribute of the serpent. Hellenistic marble statue from the large sanctuary to Asclepius on the island of Kos (2nd century B.C.). Kos, Archaeological Museum.*

*Left: the sanctuary to Asclepius at Epidaurus, part of the archaeological site.*

# HADES, LORD OF THE UNDERWORLD

Hades the son of Cronos and Rhea was the brother of Zeus, Poseidon and Hera. After the defeat of the Titans Zeus divided the rule of the cosmos among his brothers and Hades was given dominion over the Underworld, the kingdom of the dead. His control over dead souls is absolute and his will implacable, allowing no-one to return to the land of the living. In his exercise of power he is served by various demons and genii who carry out his orders (Charon the Styx ferryman is the most well known and is mentioned in Dante's *Inferno*) This malevolent god has a positive side to his nature and is also styled Pluton or Pluto ("the rich one"): as the god of the Underworld he contributes to the fertility of the earth's surface and supervises her internal riches, her wealth of minerals.

Hades rarely visits the earth and is seldom involved in the myths with the exception of his fundamental importance in the story of Demeter and Persephone. Hades became infatuated with his niece Persephone (the daughter of Zeus and Demeter) but she loved the sweet open life in the Sicilian plains. Hades determined on capturing her, which he did with the connivance of Zeus, and led her down to his kingdom. Her mother Demeter roamed the world, desperately searching for her daughter and when she learnt the name of her raptor from the Sun, who sees all, the goddess turned to Zeus. Zeus then requested that Hades release Persephone but she, ignorant of the rule forbidding those wishing to return to earth to partake of food in the Underworld, had already eaten a pomegranate seed. Zeus therefore reached a compromise with his brother so that Persephone remained part of the year with Hades and returned to her mother for the rest. This myth was offered in explanation for the changing seasons: Persephone's stay in the Underworld causing the sterility of winter while her return to the face of the earth signalled the advent of Spring.

*Hades, god of the Underworld, and Persephone. Cerberus, the guardian of the Underworld, sits at the feet of Hades. Marble Roman statue from the sanctuary of the goddess Isis at Gortyn, Crete (2nd century A.D.). Heraklion, Archaeological Museum.*

*Hades and Persephone enthroned in the kingdom of the Underworld. Terracotta votive relief, c. 470 B.C. from the sanctuary of the goddess at Locri Epizepheri (now Locri, Calabria). Reggio Calabria, National Archaeological Museum.*

# PAN, GOD OF THE PASTURE

Pan, according to some, the son of Cronos and Rhea, and to others, the son of Hermes and a nymph, is the god of shepherds and their flocks, originally worshipped in Arcadia but later in the whole of Greece and beyond. Pan is usually represented as half man and half animal: his lower half being in the shape of a goat while his upper half is like a man but with two horns sprouting from his head. His horrifying appearance caused his mother to abandon him at birth. He was found by Hermes who took him up to Olympus where he was welcomed by all the gods, especially by Dionysus who joined him to his band of satyrs (Pan had strong affinities with them in both appearance and behaviour). He often holds his Pan-pipe, made of reeds, which became the shepherds' favourite instrument. He is extremely agile, can run fast and climb nimbly over rocks. He loves to live in shady woods, often near cool streams or dense shrubbery, where he watches out for favourite nymphs and boys, or takes a lazy sleep in the midday sun much as his shepherds do. In his drive for physical contact with nymphs and youths he represents the vital force of nature, including its carnal and sexual aspects.

Pan seated on a rock, admires Aphrodite who repels his advances with a sandal. Statuette of the 3rd to 2nd century B.C. discovered near the temple of Olympian Zeus in Athens and perhaps previously in the nearby sanctuary to Pan, and a sculptural group, c. 100 B.C. from Delos. Both statues are marble. Athens, National Archaeological Museum: inv. nos. 683 and 3335.

# CHAPTER III

# THE HEROES: THE IMMORTAL VIRTUES

*Heracles, the Theban hero whose semi-divine powers symbolise man's potential redemption, attracted a vast number of stories and variety of legends. His numerous heroic actions, divided by the Greeks into "Athloi" (Twelve Labours), "Praxeis" (Gesta) and "Parerga"(Occasional deeds), were celebrated by the great poets and dramatists. Detail of a marble relief showing the hero lying on the skin of the Nemean lion, the trophy from his first labour. Athens, National Archaeological Museum.*

## HERACLES:
### SIGNS OF HIS FUTURE GREATNESS

Heracles was fathered by Zeus on a mortal, Alcmena, wife of the king of Thebes, Amphitryon. Zeus took advantage of Amphitryon's absence while fighting the war against the Teleboeans (early inhabitants of the island of Leucades) to assume his shape and conceive the most celebrated of the Greek heroes, Heracles, who because of his direct descent from Zeus, is considered a demi-god. When Amphitryon returned to discover how Zeus had deceived them it was only the direct intervention of Zeus himself that reconciled Amphitryon to his wife and made him resigned to accepting the divine child as his own. The legitimate union of the couple was also fertile, so that Alcmena bore twins, Heracles and his brother Iphicles, who was the younger by only one night as Amphitryon returned home only one day after Zeus had lain with his wife.

Even before his birth Heracles fell victim to Hera's jealousy of Alcmena. Zeus carelessly announced that the child about to be born, a descendent of Perseus (Heracles's forebears on his mother's side), would in future reign over Tirinth and Mycenae, in the region of Argos. As the births of Heracles and his cousin Eurystheus were expected at the same time Hera turned to her daughter Ilithyia, the goddess of childbirth, to delay the labour of Alcmena until the end of the tenth month and to anticipate the delivery of Eurystheus who was born after only seven months gestation. She therefore successfully contrived to make Heracles eventually subject to Eurystheus. Then when Heracles was eight months old Hera made an attempt on his life. While he slept in his cradle together with Iphicles she placed two enormous snakes beside them which proceeded to coil and entwine themselves about the infants. The terrified screams of Iphicles awoke Amphitryon who ran to the cradle his sword bared. His assistance was unnecessary as Heracles had already killed the snakes by strangling them with his bare hands. The divine origin of Heracles, in contrast to his mortal brother, was now clear. Some time later Heracles made further show of his superhuman strength: like many young men of noble lineage he was sent with his brother to study letters and music with Linus at the academy. Iphicles was a docile and hard-working student whereas Heracles was inattentive and undisciplined. One day when Linus tried to punish his unruly pupil Heracles struck him dead with his stool, or rather his lyre, as Linus had urged him to practice some exercises that he found uncongenial. Accused of murder, Heracles was absolved after a trial for having quoted a

law of Rhadamanthus, the Cretan hero and son of Zeus, renowned for his wisdom and justice. By now, however Amphitryon was afraid of the intemperate behaviour of his adopted son and determined to send him away from court, in exile to the country to watch over cattle. Heracles's education was then continued by a cowherd, a Scythian called Teutarus, who taught him the skills of archery. Others say he had other masters (Rhadamanthus himself, Eumolpus and more besides) who taught him to wield arms and perfected his musical training.

While only eighteen Heracles performed the first of his heroic undertakings when he killed the lion on Mount Cithaeron in Thebes. The lion was a monstrous and invincible beast who had destroyed many of the cattle belonging to Amphitryon and which no hunter before Heracles dared even approach. Having rid the country of this ferocious creature Heracles returned to Thebes, meeting ambassadors from the king of Orchomenos along the way. These men were also bound for Thebes to extract the tribute owed by that city to their king. Heracles attacked them, cut off their noses and ears and hung them about their necks saying that these were the tributes payable by the city of Thebes to Orchomenos. In the ensuing war waged by Orchomenos against Thebes Heracles fought beside his father Amphitryon who, although mortally wounded in battle, led his men to victory. Creon, his successor, rewarded Heracles for his leading part in the battle with the hand of his daughter Megara, who bore Heracles numerous offspring.

Heracles fell once again under the shadow of Hera's anger and she drove him in madness to kill his own children. Her plan, in these atrocious deeds was to force Heracles into the service of his cousin Eurystheus to whom he was formally subject by virtue of the unhappy prophecy made by Zeus. Heracles' horrendous crime left him so tainted and impure that he accepted with good grace to undergo any form of expiation. These were the events leading up to the twelve labours of Heracles (the *Dodekathlon*) that the hero was compelled to accept at the will of Eurysthenes, king of Tirinth and Mycenae, but in reality inspired by the jealousy of Hera.

*Heracles revealed his strong and unruly temperament at an early age when he struck his master Linus dead with his stool. He was angered by Linus insisting he practise musical exercises that the hero found unattractive. Drawing after a red-figure cup painted by the Athenian Douris c. 480 B.C., discovered in a tomb at Vulci. Munich, Antikensammlungen: inv.no. 2646.*

# THE TWELVE LABOURS (DODEKATHLON)

The story of these labours, developed from a rich epic tradition which can be traced back to the 8th century B.C, is undoubtedly based on a much earlier popular tradition. The labours became canonised as twelve in their depiction on twelve metopes (carved stone panels placed at intervals, between triglyphs on the architrave surmounting a row of columns) on the great temple to Zeus at Olympia, built about 460 B.C. The challenge posed by the Dodekathlon, which he shared with his young nephew and shield bearer, Iolaus, with the constant protection of the goddess Athene, made Heracles, more than any other classical hero, into an ideal figure. He is the personification of the highest achievements to be gained by exercising moral fortitude and physical strength in overcoming the most demoniacal and monstrous challenge even in defiance of the power of the Underworld. In completing his labours Heracles was to gain a place on Mount Olympus, where he lives in eternity in the company of the gods.

# THE NEMEAN LION

Despite a certain variation in the order of the labours all are agreed that the slaying of the lion which terrorised the plain of Nemea is the earliest. This enormous and ferocious beast was the son of the monster Echidna (the Viper with the body of a woman and a serpent's tail), and brother to the Theban Sphynx.
Heracles first attacked him with a volley of arrows, then with his club and sword, causing the bronze blade to bend at the first blow. Realising that traditional weapons were quite ineffectual against the lion's impenetrable skin Heracles approached him unarmed and, after a fierce struggle, strangled him with his bare arms. He discovered that even when dead the animal's skin remained quite invulnerable (according to Theocritus it could not be harmed by either iron or fire). To skin the beast Heracles, at the suggestion of Athene, cut him open with the animal's own gigantic claws and therefore made himself an armour pelt, the lion's head serving as a helmet.
From this time on Heracles's fundamental attribute was the Nemean lion's skin with its jaws resting over his forehead and its huge clawed paws knotted at his chest.

*Heracles fighting the mythical lion whose strength could only be overcome through unarmed combat. Roman sarcophagus of the 2nd century A.D.*
*Rome, Church of Santa Maria sopra Minerva.*

*Marble relief from Lerna,*
*2nd century B.C.*
Athens, National
Archaeological Museum: inv.
no. 3617.

# THE LERNAEAN HYDRA

Another offspring of Echidna, the terrifying Hydra, was a monster with the body of a serpent and innumerable heads (reckoned from five to one hundred and more, but generally nine) that lived in the swamps near the ancient city of Lerna. It emerged from its lair to attack herds of cattle and the region's inhabitants alike, the stench of its breath alone causing death. Heracles valiantly attacked the monster but soon realised that no sooner had one head been dispatched than another grew in its place. The combat was further complicated by the appearance of a giant crab, sent by Hera, who attacked the hero's feet. Heracles then asked for the help of his faithful sword-bearer Iolaus who set fire to the nearby forest and with the burning trunks cauterised the necks from which Heracles had struck the heads, with a razor-sharp scythe, to prevent their regrowth. He also crushed the giant crab and so returned victorious to Eurystheus at Mycenae, armed with lethal arrows which he had dipped in the poisonous blood of the Hydra.

*Athene, Heracles's protectress stands beside his four-horsed chariot as he opens combat with the Hydra. The monstrous Hydra is here shown lurking at a public fountain but more traditionally dwelt in the Lernaean marshes. Black-figure Attic hydria attributed to a painter in the circle of Leagros (510 B.C.).* Boulogne-sur-Mer, Museum.

*Archaeological site at Lerna, scene of the battle between Heracles and the monstrous Hydra. Ruins of Neolithic dwellings.*

# THE ERYMANTHIAN BOAR

The third labour imposed on Heracles by King Eurystheus was to capture alive the enormous savage boar which lived on Mount Erymanthus in Arcadia, and bring him to Mycenae. His hiding-place discovered, Heracles drove the boar into the open with loud shouts and began to chase him across the snow-covered mountains of Arcadia. He chased him until the beast was exhausted and then captured him and slung him over his shoulders to take back to the court at Mycenae. At the sight of the monstrous boar the terrified Eurystheus dived head first into one of the jars buried under ground near his throne room, and implored Heracles from his hiding place to take away the dreadful beast.

It was while engaged on this labour that Heracles rested for a time with his friend Pholus, a good Centaur who lived in a cave and fed on the raw meat of wild animals. Heracles was welcomed warmly by Pholus, who roasted meat especially for him. Heracles asked to have wine with his food but Pholus replied that he had only one jar and this was the common property of all the Centaurs on the mountain. Pholus, however, bowed to the wishes of his friend and opened the jar to serve the intoxicating wine. Its powerful aroma then filled the surrounding woods and alerted the other centaurs to the theft and they besieged the cave in a fury. In the ensuing confusion and fighting Pholus was killed by one of Heracles's poisonous arrows.

*Heracles, having captured the fierce boar which rampaged on Mount Erymanthus, carries it on his back to the court of Eurystheus. Terrorised at the sight of the beast the king took refuge in a large jar. Marble votive relief of the early 5th century B.C.* Athens, National Archaeological Museum.

*A black-figure Attic amphora (c. 510 B.C.).* Paris, Louvre. inv. no. F 59.

# THE CERYNEIAN HIND

Heracles and Pholos open the jar of wine belonging to all the centaurs, who respond furiously to the theft. Drawing after a red-figure Attic cup (500 B.C.). Basle, Antikenmuseum: inv. no. BS 489.

The fourth labour imposed on the hero was the capture of the Hind of Cerynaea. The large animal, bigger than a bull with golden horns like a stag, was one of a herd of five that the goddess Artemis found grazing while out hunting. She caught four of them to harness to her chariot while the fifth ran free to Mount Cerynaea on the borders of Achaea and Arcadia. Heracles followed the swift creature for one whole year without every coming close to her (some say the chase took him as far as Istria and the northern lands of the Hyperboreans).

Finally tired, the hind rested by a river where Heracles captured her, having lightly wounded her with one of his arrows. Carrying her on his shoulders he started his return journey to the court of Eurystheus but was met by Artemis and her twin Apollo who sought to reclaim the hind as sacred to the cult of the huntress, and accused Heracles of sacrilege. Heracles pleaded necessity, being compelled in this labour by Eurystheus, so that he was forgiven and allowed to carry the hind alive to Mycenae.

*Heracles attacks the magic hind with golden horns which ran wild on Mount Cerynaea. The enormous, swift and powerful beast was sacred to Artemis, but she forgave Heracles for capturing the hind as he was compelled in this labour by Eurystheus. Marble metope from the Athenian Treasury at Delphi (shortly after 490 B.C.). Delphi, Archaeological Museum, Metope no. 19.*

*The Athenian Treasury. A small building in the form of a Doric temple, with a two-columned portico, decorated with carved metopes illustrating the labours of Heracles, was built in the sanctuary of Apollo at Delphi shortly after 490 B.C. (though some put its construction prior to 500 B.C.). It was probably built to commemorate the famous victory of the Athenians over the Persians, at Marathon, and also to house part of the rich booty captured by the Greeks, given as a votive offering to Apollo.*

*View of the wild Erymanthian mountain landscape, in Arcadia, the scene of the devastation wrecked by the monstrous boar, named after the mountain. The boar was captured live by Heracles and taken to the court of the cowardly Eurystheus who threw himself head first into a jar at the sight of the savage beast.*

# THE STYMPHALIAN BIRDS

In a thick, dark forest beside the marshes surrounding the Stymphalian lake in Arcadia there lived an enormous flock of birds who had migrated there to escape an invasion of wolves. They bred at an extraordinary rate and had wonderful variegated metallic feathers so sharp that they speared to death any who came near them. They were a great plague to the surrounding countryside as they destroyed and devoured the local inhabitants as well as devastating crops and stripping the trees of fruit. Eurystheus sent Heracles to exterminate them and his first difficulty was to drive them from the dark forest. It was his protectress Athene who devised the successful stratagem: her faithful ally Hephaestus, the smith-god, forged a bronze clapper to startle the birds and force them to take flight. The unexpected sounding of the clapper sent the birds into disarray and Heracles swiftly brought them down with his arrows.

Views of lake Stymphalos, now just a short stretch of water, but once a large lake surrounded by forests and marshes. This was the dwelling place of the enormous flock of savage birds brought down by Heracles, acting on the advice of Athene. In her willingness to help the hero, the goddess asked Hephaestus, the god of fire, to forge a bronze clapper for Heracles. The startled birds were then forced from their forest hiding place into the open where Heracles swiftly exterminated them and rid the whole area of the dangerous and destructive creatures.

*Crete: view in the direction of Balion, delightful bay on the north coast (above), and the north-east coast near Siteia. The seventh labour of Heracles, the capture of the fierce bull who was devastating the island, was achieved by the heroin Crete.*

# THE AUGEIAN STABLES

Augeias, son of Helius and king of Elis, where the great sanctuary to Zeus at Olympia stands, had many herds of cattle as a gift from his father but constantly neglected the cleaning of their stables which grew more filthy every day. Not only were the animals forced to live in the most insalubrious conditions but the surrounding countryside was deprived of valuable fertiliser and was totally unproductive. When Eurystheus ordered Heracles to clean the stables, Augeias was delighted and made a wager with the hero: if the labour were completed in a day Augeias would present Heracles with a tenth of his herds. Heracles made a breach in the stable walls and diverted the waters of two nearby rivers, the Alpheus and the Peneus, through the stables and the yard, washing all the filth away in one day. Augeias was infuriated by Heracles's victory and refused to hand over the promised quota of cattle until his own son Phyleus testified to the agreement and brought about a just settlement.

# THE CRETAN BULL

His seventh labour, the first accomplished outside the Peloponnese, found Heracles in Crete where he was to capture a ferocious bull of extraordinary strength. It is disputed whether this bull was the same that brought Europa to the island, galloping over the waves (this version is favoured by those who do not consider that the bull was Zeus himself, transformed for the seduction of Europa) or the fine beast who captivated Pasiphaë, wife of King Minos, and sired the Minotaur, the same bull who had appeared miraculously from the sea the day Minos promised to sacrifice to Poseidon whatever emerged from the waves. When Minos saw the beauty of the beast he decided to make him one of his own herd and sacrificed a different bull to Poseidon. Enraged at the deceit, Poseidon made the bull run in fury and devastation throughout the island until it was captured by Heracles with his lasso. Heracles presented the bull to Eurystheus, who wanted to consecrate it to Hera, but the goddess was reluctant to accept any offering which reflected glory on Heracles and so released the bull to roam wild in Greece. It reached the plains of Marathon before its final capture by Theseus.

*The hero's unique and semi-divine strength meant that he alone could cleanse the stables belonging to King Augeias, the son of Helius, in a single day. Colossal statue of Heracles, known as the Heracles Farnese (2nd century A.D.) from the Baths of Caracalla in Rome. Naples, National Archaeological Museum.*

# THE MARES OF DIOMEDES

Diomedes, according to some the son of Ares, was king of Thrace, the wild region on the shores of the Black Sea. He kept four savage mares tethered with iron chains to a bronze manger; they fed on the flesh of any unsuspecting visitor who chanced to travel in the kingdom. Heracles, charged with the labour of taming these animals, left for distant Thrace where he captured Diomedes and fed him to his own mares, thereby gaining control over them. He then led them meekly to the court of Eurystheus, who dedicated them to Hera and set them free near Mycenae, where, it is said, the breed survived until the time of Alexander the Great.

Another account relates how Heracles went to Thrace accompanied by a group of volunteers to help him with this most perilous task. Abderus, a youth of whom Heracles was particularly fond, was one of the party. Heracles captured the mares with ease but when pursued by Diomedes and his troops left Abderus with the beasts while he fought the enemy. The inexperienced Abderus was eaten by the mares. Heracles then fed Diomedes to his beasts, who became calm, and then saw to the worthy burial of Abderus and founded the city of Abdera beside his tomb.

*To tame the flesh-eating mares belonging to Diomedes, the king of Thrace and son of Ares, Heracles had to overpower their master. While Heracles fought Diomedes, the beasts ate the hero's young companion, Abderus, in whose memory Heracles founded the nearby city of Abdera. Drawing after the decoration inside a black-figure on coral cup attributed to the great Athenian painter Psiax (c. 510 B.C.). St Petersburg, Hermitage Museum.*

# HIPPOLYTE'S GIRDLE

The Amazons were female warriors who only kept their female offspring and amputated their right breast to suckle their young from the left, so as not to obstruct shooting from the bow or the throw of the spear. They lived in the distant and mysterious lands of the north on the slopes of the Caucasus with Temiscyra as their capital. The bravest of all was Hippolyte, their queen, also the daughter of Ares, who had given her a precious girdle, a symbol of the absolute power she held over her people. Admete, the daughter of Eurystheus, asked Heracles to organise an expedition against the Amazons and to capture the celebrated girdle. The hero armed a ship and set sail with several volunteers including Theseus and Telamon. When they reached Temiscyra at the mouth of the river Thermodon, the heroes were welcomed by the Amazons, and Hippolyte would willingly have yielded her girdle to Heracles had not the jealous Hera sewn the seeds of discord between the two parties. Having taken on the appearance of one of the female warriors, Hera spread the rumour among the Amazons that Heracles had come to steal their queen. A fierce battle broke out which concluded with the death of Hippolyte at the hand of Heracles, who then stole the girdle to carry back to Admete.

It was during the return voyage that what became known as the first Trojan War took place. Laomedon, then king of Troy, offended the gods Apollo and Poseidon, who were helping him build the city, refusing to give them the marvellous horses he had received from Zeus, and which he had promised the gods as a reward for their assistance. It was after the construction of the city walls, the finest ever seen, that Laomedon refused the gods their prize, causing Poseidon to send a sea-monster against Troy and Apollo a plague. These hardships would only disappear with the sacrifice of Hesione, Laomedon's daughter to the sea-monster. The intervention of Heracles led to the slaying of the sea-monster and the marriage of the beautiful Hesione to his companion in arms Telamon.

Laomedon and all his sons were then killed in retribution but Heracles spared the youngest son, Podarces ("swift-foot") at the request of Hesione in exchange for a beautiful veil which she herself had embroidered with gold. From that time the young prince was called Priam (meaning "bought" or "ransomed") and he became the most famous of the kings of Troy.

## THE CATTLE OF GERYON

Geryon, the monstrous son of Chrysaor and therefore a nephew of the Gorgon, had the appearance of a warrior with three bodies joined together at the waist, and lived on the island of Erytheia in the far west of the world. He owned enormous herds of cattle, watched over by the herdsman Eurytion and the watchdog Orthrus. Eurystheus ordered Heracles to capture the cattle, killing both their guardians and their owner.

The difficulties posed by this tenth labour were considerable, the first problem being the crossing of the ocean. Heracles having crossed the Libyan desert was so upset by the great heat that he strung his bow and shot an arrow at the sun. Helius protested and Heracles promised to shoot no more if the Sun would lend him his great golden goblet which the god sailed in every evening to his home in the east, and in this the hero sailed to Erytheia. On his arrival he was attacked by the two-headed Orthrus, whom he dispatched with a blow of his club. He then fought with Eurythion who had come to the aid of his dog, and he was also overcome before Heracles tackled Geryon whose three bodies were torn asunder. Heracles then ferried the cattle in Helius's goblet across the ocean to the court of Eurystheus, where they were sacrificed to Hera.

*Heracles in combat with the three-bodied monster Geryon. Drawing after an embossed bronze shield band, c. 550 B.C. from the sanctuary of Zeus at Olympia. Olympia, Archaeological Museum: inv. no. B 1975.*

*Black-figure Attic hydria painted by Lydos (c. 560 B.C.). Rome, National Etruscan Museum, Villa Giulia.*

*Heracles in the presence of his protectress, the goddess Athene, attempts to calm Cerberus, the fierce guardain of the Underworld, in order to capture him. Drawing after the red-figure Attic amphora decorated on both sides by the painter known as the Painter of Andokides (c. 520 B.C.). Paris, Louvre: inv. no. F 204.*

*Heracles battles with the sea-god Nereus in an attempt to force him to reveal the whereabouts of the garden of the Hesperides. Drawing after an embossed bronze shield band, c. 550 B.C. from the sanctuary of Zeus at Olympia. Olympia, Archaeological Museum: inv. no. B 1881d.*

## THE CAPTURE OF CERBERUS

The eleventh labour imposed on Heracles by Eurystheus was to descend to the Underworld and capture Cerberus, the giant dog guarding the kingdom of the Dead, who prevented the living from entering and, with even greater vigilance, the dead from leaving. Generally depicted with two or more heads, a snake's tail and a ridge of snake heads down his back, Cerberus would never have been taken without the aid of the gods. Heracles was first initiated into the Mysteries at Eleusis, learning how to emerge unscathed from the land of the Beyond, then, with the help of Hermes and Athene he descended into the realm of Hades who granted him permission to take Cerberus with him to the land of the living if he could do so without the use of any weapon. Heracles wrestled with the animal with his bare arms and overpowered him. He brought the huge creature to Mycenae, where Eurystheus was terrified at the sight of him, and at a loss to know what to do with his prize asked Heracles to return the creature to the Underworld.

While in the Underworld Heracles met Theseus and Pirithous who had been punished by Hades in their attempt to lead Persephone back to the face of the earth and were chained to a rock. Heracles freed Theseus but Pirithous had to remain in the Underworld on account of his arrogance.

## THE APPLES OF THE HESPERIDES

The last labour Heracles had to undertake was to gather fruit from the golden apple-tree of the Hesperides, the Nymphs of the evening. Mother Earth had given Hera some golden apples in celebration of her marriage to Zeus, and Hera was so delighted with them that she planted them in her garden, near Mount Atlas in the far west of the world. As the daughters of Atlas would secretly enter the garden to steal ap-

*Heracles freeing the titan Prometheus from where he was chained to a mountain in the Caucasus and had his liver eaten daily by the eagle sent by Zeus. Drawing after an Attic krater attributed to the Painter of Nessos (c.610 B.C.). Athens, National Archaeological Museum: inv. no. 16384.*

*Heracles, with his arms laid aside, struggles with the giant Antaeus who can only be defeated if lifted with bare hands from the earth, his mother, from which he drew his strength. The combat is witnessed by Athene, in support of Heracles, and by another divine figure, perhaps Gaia, who already bemoans the fate of Antaeus. Drawing after a black-figure hydria (c. 510 B.C.). Boulogne-sur-Mer, Museum.*

ples from the miraculous tree Hera placed an immortal monster with one hundred heads, the son of Echidna, to guard it. Heracles's greatest difficulty was to discover exactly where the garden was to be found but he set out towards the sea and in Thessaly fought and killed Cycnus, the son of Ares, who had for long slain passers-by and travellers, offering their flesh in sacrifice to his father. In Illyria, beside the waters of the Erydanus Heracles met the nymphs of the river who told him that only the river-god Nereus would be able to direct him to the garden. Heracles was led before Nereus who refused to give him directions whereupon Heracles caught him in a vice-like grip, from which Nereus tried unsuccessfully to escape by assuming a variety of forms but was eventually forced to reveal the way to the garden of the Hesperides.

Heracles continued his journey through Libya where he met, and killed, the giant Antaeus, the son of Poseidon, who forced travellers into combat with him then adorned his father's temple with their battered remains. In Egypt the vilely cruel King Busiris had put Heracles in chains in preparation for his ritual sacrifice when Heracles burst his fetters, tore off the sacred bands and slew Busiris and his attendants. During his travels in the Caucasus Heracles had also liberated the titan Prometheus who had been chained to a rock by Zeus where daily his liver was pecked at by vultures only to regrow over night. In gratitude Prometheus told Heracles that he must not take the apples by himself but seek help from Atlas, brother to Prometheus. Heracles, when he arrived at the garden went straight to Atlas who, as a divine punishment, was obliged to carry the earth on his shoulders. Heracles offered to relieve Atlas of his great burden if he would gather three of the golden apples from the garden of the Hesperides for him. The task completed Atlas was unwilling to take the weight of the world on his shoulders again and offered to take the apples to Eurystheus himself. Heracles feigned agreement but asked Atlas to shoulder his burden again for a moment while he made himself more comfortable with a cushion to support the weight. The unsuspecting Atlas resumed his former role and Heracles was free to return to Mycenae. Eurystheus took the three apples, but once he had admired their beauty he had no idea what to do with them and gave them back to Heracles, who in turn gave them to his constant advisor and supporter, Athene. She brought them back to the Hesperides as divine law ordained that they remain in the garden of the gods.

*Heracles takes the burden of the heavens momentarily from the titan Atlas and in return Atlas brings him the magical apples from the garden of the Hesperides. Metope from the temple of Zeus at Olympia, carved c. 460 B.C. by the Master of Olympia.* Olympia, Archaeological Museum: metope no. 10.

*Heracles kills Busiris and his Egyptian priests on the altar where they intended to sacrifice the hero. The Egyptians are easily recognisable as they are circumcised, and have shaven heads and negroid features. Red-figure pelike, c. 460 B.C. by the Athenian painter usually known as the Pan Painter.* Athens, National Archaeological Museum: inv. no. 9683.

# LOVE AFTER THE LABOURS: DEIANEIRA AND THE STORY OF NESSUS

The lovely Deianeira was the daughter of Oeneus, king of Calydon, and her marriage to Heracles was prophesied by her ghost brother Meleager during Heracles's descent to the Underworld. Deianeira's two most pressing suitors were Heracles and the river-god Achelous, who appeared as a bull with a human face. Heracles was forced into exile from Calydon for having unwittingly killed one of Oeneus's relations, and took Deianeira with him to the banks of the Evenus, where the centaur Nessus acted as ferryman. Having taken Heracles across the river, Nessus returned for Deianeira but far from carrying her across, attempted to violate her. Heracles took his bow and shot Nessus with one of his arrows. The dying Nessus thought of his revenge: he told Deianeira how to mix a love potion from the blood dripping from his wound in order to ensure the continuous fidelity of Heracles. Deianeira, suspecting no guile, collected the blood. Some time later Heracles became infatuated with Iole, the daughter of Eurytus, king of Oechalia, and repudiated Deianeira who, mindful of Nessus's potion, dipped one of Heracles's tunics in the liquid. The hero was immediately seized with the violent effects of the lethal poison, and begged his followers to place him on a pyre in preparation for his death.

*Heracles kills the centaur Nessus by plunging his sword between his shoulders having first secured him by placing his foot on his back. Nessus had attempted to violate Heracles's wife, Deianeira. Monumental black-figure Attic funerary amphora, painted c. 600 B.C. by the Painter of Nessus.* Athens, National Archaeological Museum: inv. no. 1002.

# THE APOTHEOSIS OF HERACLES: A HERO AMONG THE GODS

All were loth to place the tormented Heracles on the funeral pyre as instructed, except Philoctetes who obeyed the hero with resignation. A high pyre was built and Heracles placed on top of it before Philoctetes set it alight. In recognition of his painful fidelity Heracles presented him with his bow and arrows. No sooner had the fire started to burn than Athene appeared from the heavens in her chariot and took up the hero to transport him to their father Zeus on Mount Olympus. There he lived with the immortals, and reconciled with Hera, who was mindful of his role in the battle against the Giants, received the gift of eternal youth from Zeus and was given Hera's pretty daughter, Hebe, the cup-bearer of the gods, in marriage.

*Above: Heracles at a banquet at the court of King Eurytus, where he fell in love with Iole, causing him to repudiate Deianeira, his legitimate wife. Drawing after a black-figure krater with small columns produced in Corinth, c. 600 B.C. Paris, Louvre: inv. no. E 635.*

*Right: detail of a sculpted pediment c. 580 B.C. from a temple on the Acropolis at Athens depicting Heracles in combat with the sea-monster Triton. Athens, Acropolis Museum.*

# JASON, MEDEA AND THE ADVENTURES OF THE ARGONAUTS

## PHRYGIUS AND HELLE

Athamas, son of the god of the wind, Aeolus, had as his first wife Nephele ("cloud") who bore him two sons, Phrygius ("pelting rain") and Helle ("bright light"). He later became infatuated with Ino, the beautiful daughter of the king of Thebes, Cadmos, and abandoned Nephele who in revenge sent a terrible drought over the land. Ino tried to persuade Athamas to sacrifice the children of his first marriage in an attempt to placate the divine wrath manifest in the infliction of the drought. Nephele then intervened to spare her offspring giving them a ram with a golden fleece which she had received in gift from Hermes. Phrygius and Helle were therefore able to escape the cruelty of their step-mother and mounted on the magical ram fled to Colchis, the wild region to the east of the Euxine or Black Sea. While crossing the waves however Helle lost her grip of the ram and fell into the sea (*ponto* in Greek) known as the Hellespont ever since. When Phrygius reached Colchis he sacrificed the ram to Zeus, the protector of fugitives, and hung the bright fleece in the wood sacred to Ares, placing a terrible dragon to watch over it.

# JASON AND PELIAS

It was this same golden fleece that Pelias, Jason's usurping uncle asked his nephew to bring him in order to prove his worth as the successor to the throne of Iolcus. The throne was in fact Jason's rightful inheritance, as his father, Aeson, had been deposed by Pelias when Jason was a baby. Brought up and educated by the centaur Chiron, Jason returned to Iolcus dressed in strange apparel with a leopard skin and only one sandal while Pelias was officiating at a public sacrifice. Pelias when he saw Jason failed to recognise him as his nephew, but was reminded of the ancient prophecy pronouncing his overthrow by a man with one sandal. He therefore challenged Jason with the seizure of the golden fleece, confident that he would be killed in the attempt.

# THE LONG JOURNEY OF THE ARGO

Jason sent a messenger throughout Greece and recruited volunteers from among the great heroes of his time. He armed a ship, known as the Argo after its shipwright and meaning "swift-sailing"; its crew became known as the Argonauts, and included seers with powers of premonition. The vessel too had the gift of prophesy, as its prow had been carved by Athene herself from an oak tree taken from the wood sacred to Zeus beside his sanctuary at Dodona.

Following numerous perilous adventures, none of which is depicted in classical art, taking her heroic company to the shores of the most varied lands and to the strangest people, the Argo reached Colchis. Here they received a warm welcome from King Aeëtes, who mindful of Pelias's challenge was willing to consign the fleece as long as Jason, without any help, could yoke two fire-breathing bulls with bronze hooves and plough and sow a field with dragon's teeth.

*The divine intervention of Athene causes the dragon, placed to guard the magic golden fleece, to regurgitate Jason. Drawing after the central tondo, red-figure cup painted c. 470 B.C. by the Athenian painter Douris. Rome, Vatican Museums: inv. No. 16545.*

# MEDEA: ENCHANTMENT AND LOVE

Jason would have found the tasks set him by Aeëtes impossible if not for the assistance given him by the king's daughter, the witch-priestess Medea. She fell deeply in love with Jason and prepared a potion for him to make both his body and his weapons invincible when under attack from the bulls and from the warriors who were to rise armed from the dragon's teeth when sown in the field. Medea also warned Jason of this particular danger in advance and told him how to defeat the warriors by throwing a stone quoit to set them fighting one against the other in fatal combat.

Jason promised Medea undying love and matrimony in return for her aid in securing the golden fleece. As they fled away together, Aeëtes followed in desperate pursuit but was obliged to stop along the way to gather up the limbs of his dismembered son, Apsyrtus, and prepare his body for burial. The youth had been cut into pieces by Medea purposely to distract Aeëtes.

Zeus, angered by the barbaric murder of Apsyrtus, hurled down a howling tempest sending the Argo off course. The ship with her oracular powers revealed to the Argonauts that the anger of the father of all the gods would not be appeased until the murderers had been purified by the witch Circe, Medea's own aunt. Circe performed the necessary purification but failed to offer them hospitality. The ship then headed again for the open sea and visited the straits of Messina, Sicily, Corfu, Crete, Aegina and Euboea before returning, after months of navigation, to Iolcus.

*Medea demonstrates her rejuvenating potion to the daughters of Pelias by boiling a ram in a large cauldron, and persuades them to try the same treatment on their father. The enchantress so punished Pelias for not keeping his promise to resign his kingdom to Jason following the successful return of his expedition. Drawing after a black-figure Attic hydria painted c. 510 B.C. London, British Museum: inv. no. B. 328.*

## THE RETURN TO IOLCUS

When Jason returned to Pelias with the golden fleece the treacherous king refused to keep his promise to resign the throne. Once again it was Medea who helped the hero at his time of greatest need. She persuaded the daughters of Pelias that if they cut him to pieces and boiled him in a large bronze cauldron together with one of her magic potions he would be restored to life with renewed youth and vitality. And so Pelias was successfully dispatched, but Jason and Medea were forced to flee from Iolcus to Corinth to escape the vengeance of Pelias's son, Acastus.

At Corinth, where Jason dedicated the Argo to Poseidon in his sanctuary on the isthmus, the hero fell in love with Glauce, the daughter of King Creon, and repudiated Medea. To wreak her revenge Medea sent the bride a poisoned robe and diadem provoking her death the instant she tried them on. Driven to madness in his sorrow Jason turned against Medea but she anticipated his violence and killed two of their sons before retreating to the heavens in a wonderful chariot sent by the Sun.

# THESEUS, THE ATHENIAN HERO

Held by some to be the son of Poseidon, Theseus, the Athenian hero *par excellence*, was the son of Aegeus, king of Athens, and of Aethra, the daughter of Pittheus, king of Troezen in the Peloponnese. Theseus passed his early years in the care of his grandfather, in Troezen, as Aegeus was fearful for his safety among his jealous cousins, the fifty sons of Pallas, who had designs upon the throne. Before leaving Theseus in Troezen Aegeus hid his sword and sandals under an enormous rock, telling only Aethra of their whereabouts, to be revealed to Theseus when he was strong enough to lift the rock, retrieve his father's gifts, and return to Athens.

*Above, the archaeological site at the sanctuary of Poseidon at Isthmia, near the isthmus cut to form the Corinth canal. Traditionally this is the spot where Jason dedicated his boat, the Argo, when he returned from his expedition.*

*Right, the agora in Corinth dominated by the impressive monolithic doric columns of the temple of Apollo.*

# THESEUS'S JOURNEY TO ATHENS

Grown to manhood and eager to return to Athens, Theseus was told to be careful by his mother Aethra and his grandfather Pittheus, who advised him against making the journey overland. But as Heracles, the great hero of the Peloponnese, had been absent for some time the roads were once again infested with brigands and monsters. Theseus was keen to emulate the fame of his celebrated companion and chose to travel the infested highways rather than sail the safety of the seas. At Epidaurus he met Periphetes, the deformed son of Hephaestus, who walked with the support of a bronze club with which he struck dead those who came near him. Theseus slew him and took possession of his club which from then on became his favourite weapon.

The hero freed the isthmus of its troubles, killing the brigand Sinis with the same torture he had inflicted on so many travellers: he would ambush men and tie them to the extremities of two pine trees bent close together by force; these released would split the poor victims in two.

In the forest of Crommyum Theseus fought the fierce wild sow who had brought destruction to many Crommyonians and their harvests. She was thought to be one of the monstrous offspring of Typhon and Echidna, and therefore the sister of Cerberus, Orthrus, the Chimera, the Lernaean Hydra, and of the dragon who guarded the golden fleece and of the monster set in watch over the apples in the garden of the Hesperides. The sow was also the half-sister of the Nemean lion, born of the incestuous union between Echidna and her son Orthrus. Theseus killed the sow, called Phea after the old woman who kept her, with the sword left him by his father Aegeus under the rock at Troezen.

At an extremely narrow point of the Isthmus of Corinth, near Megara, Theseus came across Sciron, the bandit, the son of Poseidon, who was in the habit of asking travellers to wash his feet and then kicking them into the sea below when they bent down to perform the operation; in the sea they were soon devoured by a giant turtle.

*Drawing after a red-figure cup showing the deeds of Theseus painted by the Athenian Douris (c. 470 B.C.) and discovered at Vulci. To the left: Theseus attacks the Crommyum sow while Phea, the old woman who kept her, tries to restrain him. To the right: Theseus punishes the brigand Sinis with the same torture he himself had inflicted on others.*
London, British Museum: inv. no. E 48.

Theseus treated Sciron as he had treated former victims and so the pass was rid of this barbaric practice.

Near Eleusis, not far from the Megarean border, Theseus defeated the giant Cercyon who obliged passers-by to engage him in physical combat, and then crushed them to death. Despite the marked difference in their size Theseus showed superior skill in their struggle and, lifting the giant above his head, smashed him violently upside down to the ground, crushing his skull.

Continuing on the road from Megara to Athens, Theseus came to the house of Procrustes (also known as Damastes), who tortured travellers on his beds, one short and one long. Tall travellers were forced to lie on the shorter bed and had their extremities trimmed to fit the couch, while shorter victims had their limbs stretched to fit the longer bed. In this case too Theseus defeated the torturer by making him a victim to his own torture.

After the courageous execution of so many labours, involving so many deaths, Theseus had to be purified by the priests on the banks of the Cephissus in Attica before approaching the throne of his father Aegeus in Athens. At his father's court he did not make his identity known immediately, as he realised that the king was under the magic power of Medea, who, according to some versions, had come to Athens from Corinth to escape the vengeance of Jason. Medea however recognised Theseus immediately and devised a plan to be rid of him and so smoothe the succession of the fifty sons of Pallas, eager to assume government of the kingdom of Aegea, which they held to be without heirs. Just as Theseus was about to drink the potion she had prepared for him, Aegeus recognised the sword and sandals that he had hidden in Troezen so long ago and knocked the poisoned chalice from his hand in his embrace. Her plot discovered, Medea fled and the cousins were for the most part killed or driven into exile.

*Theseus, in the presence of Athene, punishes the brigands Sciron and Cercyon. Sciron was thrown down from the cliff where previously he had thrown those victims whom he had forced to wash his feet. Theseus crushed Cercyon to death in physical combat as the brigand had crushed so many passers-by before. Drawing after the B side of the cup on the previous page.*

# THESEUS IN CRETE

Theseus then stayed with his father, the undisputed sovereign of Athens. The city was oppressed by the heavy tribute demanded by Minos, king of Crete, who every nine years awaited the arrival of seven young men and seven maidens from Athens who, after their arrival in Crete were fed to the monstrous son of Minos, the Minotaur, a man with the head of a bull who dwelt in the fearsome labyrinth. Theseus when the time came asked to be numbered among those sent to Crete, intent on liberating his city from such a shameful practice. He told his sad father that should his mission prove successful the returning ship would unfurl white sails, otherwise they would remain black, like those on the sorrowful outward journey.

Aphrodite intervened to help Theseus by making Ariadne, Minos's lovely daughter, fall deeply in love with him. She was strolling on the beach with her nurse when she saw the ship laden with the young Athenians arrive. Struck by the courage of their leader Theseus, she determined to help him by showing him how to find his way out of the labyrinth. Ariadne gave him a ball of wool which he slowly unravelled as he penetrated the complex corridors of the labyrinth until he found the dreadful Minotaur which he killed with his sword before returning, by rewinding the thread, to Ariadne, waiting anxiously for him outside.

Theseus then fled back to his ship with Ariadne, to whom he made promises of eternal love, and they embarked for Athens together with all the young Athenians who had escaped the monstrous sacrifice.

They stopped on their journey on the island of Naxos where Ariadne fell asleep on the beach. Theseus then made the treacherous decision to abandon her and return directly to Attica (others say a violent storm hastily drove the ship away from Naxos before Ariadne could re-embark). When Ariadne awoke and realised her fate she sank into despair, but was soon distracted by the arrival of Dionysus and his festive chariot drawn by panthers. The god fell deeply in love with her and led her away in his chariot to Mount Olympus where he made her his bride and obtained the gift of immortality for her from Zeus.

Theseus in the meantime drew close to Athens but, intoxicated by his success, forgot to unfurl the white sails he had promised his father Aegeus. Aegeus had kept watch every day for the return of the Athenian ship and when he saw the black sails approaching imagined

*Marble torso of the Minotaur, the monster slain by the hero, Theseus. Athens, National Archaeological Museum.*

*Theseus holds the Minotaur to the ground and prepares to inflict a mortal blow as the monster raises a hand as if imploring mercy. Red-figure Attic pelike, c. 480 B.C. Rome, Vatican Museums.*

that all the young Athenians and his own beloved
son had been fed to the Minotaur. In despair he threw himself head first into the sea which
has been named after him ever
since. He fell from the Acropolis,
where even today below the walls supporting the small temple of Athene are two
niches recording the father's death.

## THE FURTHER ADVENTURES OF THESEUS

As lord of Athens and Attica Theseus is best remembered for having united the various regions of Attica into a single community and for having founded the "Pan-
Athenian" games, great religious festivities in honour of the goddess Athene in which
all the regions participated with games, ceremonies, processions, parades and races.
Nevertheless he still had many ordeals to undergo and difficulties to overcome, some
bringing him great fame, such as the war against the Amazons. Theseus was power-
fully attracted by the proud female warriors and set out on a journey to their capital
at Temiscyra. When he arrived he was given a friendly welcome by their queen who
sent Antiope with precious gifts for the new guest. Theseus then invited the beautiful amazon on board his ship, and set sail with his prey. The Amazons then invaded
Attica to recover Antiope advancing as far as Athens and engaging in bitter conflict
with the army led by Theseus. Theseus and his forces eventually put one wing of the
Amazon army to flight so that the women were forced to make peace.
Antiope bore Theseus Hippolytus but the hero then became infatuated with the lovely Phaedra, the daughter of Minos and sister to Ariadne. In order to marry her Theseus repudiated Antiope but kept the young Hippolytus, who grew strong and brave
like his father. His step-mother Phaedra fell in love with him, but when rebuffed by
Hippolytus she accused him of making attempts on her virtue and had him punished
by Theseus. Theseus asked Dionysus to administer punishment and he sent down a
wild bull which emerged unexpectedly from the waves frightening the horses pulling

*After they had fled from Crete, Theseus and Ariadne rested on the island of Naxos where Athene appeared to the hero at dead of night and insisted on his immediate return to Athens. The unsuspecting Ariadne lies asleep with the small figure of Hypnos, Sleep, curled up above her head. Red-figure Attic lekythos painted c. 480 B.C. Taranto, Archaeological Museum.*

Hippolytus's chariot. They then ran amok dragging the youth along by the reins and battering him to death.

Theseus still had many brave feats to accomplish, including the capture of a ferocious bull who breathed fire from his nostrils and ran wild in the plain of Marathon, destroying crops and attacking peasants (it is sometimes thought that this is the same bull Heracles brought from Crete to Eurystheus, who was terrified and let it free).

In his old age Theseus resigned the throne of Athens to Menestheus as the political climate had turned against him. He took refuge on the island of Scyros at the court of King Lycomedes, a relative who appeared to receive him warmly. After his reception the king led Theseus to the top of a high hill on the pretext of showing him the splendid view of the island but Lycomedes threw Theseus to his death.

During the battle of Marathon (490 B.C.), in the war between the Greeks and the Persians, the Athenian soldiers reported being led by a hero of magnificent stature who they recognised as Theseus. At the end of the war Cimon, the Athenian statesman, consulted the Delphic oracle who ordered him to retrieve the bones of Theseus and bring them back to Athens. Cimon then conquered the island of Scyros and having sighted an eagle at the top of a hill scraping the earth with its talons, he recognised it as an augury and excavated the spot to discover a tomb containing the bones of a warrior, a bronze spear and a sword. The bones were brought back to Athens and fêted in a manner worthy of a god.

*Athens, Acropolis: two niches at the base of the bastion beneath the small temple to the Athenian Nike. This is held to be the site of the ritual worship of Aegeus, the father of Theseus, who fell to this spot from the Acropolis when he saw the approach of the black sails, signalling the death of his son and the failure of the expedition against the Minotaur.*

# PERSEUS AND MEDUSA

Acrisius, king of Argolis, had enclosed his daughter Danae in an impenetrable bronze chamber underground in an attempt to prevent the fulfilment of a prophecy, proclaiming his overthrow by his own grandson. Zeus, however, enamoured of the beautiful maiden, visited her in a shower of gold and so Danae conceived Perseus. The cries of the baby alerted Acrisius to his birth and he abandoned both mother and child to the waves, enclosing them in a wooden ark.

The two were washed ashore on the island of Seriphos, were they were welcomed by King Polydectes. As Perseus grew he protected his mother from the advances of Polydectes and the king, to rid himself of this unwelcome interference, charged him with the dangerous task of finding the Gorgons and of killing the only mortal one, Medusa. Perseus received the help of both Hermes and Athene who gave him advice and invaluable aids to ensure the success of the enterprise: winged sandals offering him a swift retreat, a sack to carry the evil head of the Medusa and a helmet rendering him invisible.

Perseus then sought out the three Graeae, sisters to the Gorgons, hideous and decrepit in appearance having been born old, who had only one tooth and one eye between them which they passed around. Perseus managed to snatch the eye from them and would only restore it when the Graeae had revealed the whereabouts of their sisters.

When Perseus reached the hideaway of the three Gorgons (Stheno, Euryale and Medusa) he found them asleep. These monstrous sisters had necks covered in dragon scales, wild boar tusks, brazen hands and golden wings but most fearsome of all

*Medusa with her two sons (who were born from the blood of her severed head), Chrysaor and Pegasus. Drawing after embossed bronze shield band, c. 620 B.C. from Olympia. Olympia, Archaeological Museum: inv. no. 1911c.*

*The Gorgoneion, or head of Medusa, decapitated by Perseus, with her serpent hair petrified those who beheld her. Her head was used as an emblem on the centre of shields to terrify the enemy as well as as a apotropaic symbol. Mosaic pavement (2nd century A.D.). Athens, National Archaeological Museum.*

*Facing page: Perseus in the presence of his protectress, Athene, decapitates the Gorgon, turning his head away to avoid being turned into stone. The blood from the Gorgon's head has already given birth to one of her children, Pegasus, the winged horse, but Chrysaor is not yet born. Limestone metope from Selinus (c.530 B.C.). Palermo, National Archaeological Museum.*

were their locks of writhing serpents and their very looks had the power of petrifying all those who beheld them. Perseus to avoid Medusa's direct gaze watched her in the polished bronze shield held up for him by Athene. He cut off her head, deposited in the magic bag, put on his helmet rendering him invisible and took flight immediately to escape the wrath of the two immortal sisters. Perseus left their cave and flew to safety while two streams of blood flowed copiously from the Medusa's head: the left, malign spurt was lethal poison while the right, benign spurt, was collected by Athene and given to Asclepius to cure the sick although he also used it to revive the dead. The blood shed by Medusa also gave birth to her children, the winged horse Pegasus, later tamed by Bellerophon to fight against the Chimera, and the warrior Chrysaor, the "youth with the golden sword". Medusa's head was later given to Athene, and she wore it on her aegis, the invulnerable goatskin from Amalthea which served as her armour.

While speeding home with his trophy Perseus spied a girl of wondrous beauty, Andromeda, the daughter of Cepheus and Cassiopeia who reigned in Ethiopia. As Cassiopeia had offended the Nereids, the

*Perseus looks away to avoid being turned to stone as he kills the Gorgon, Medusa, holding her by her serpent locks and passing the blade of the sword through her neck. He is assisted by his protectress, the goddess Athene, who appears to be holding the Gorgon by the shoulder as well as by her locks. Drawing after an embossed bronze shield band, c. 590 B.C. from the sanctuary of Zeus at Olympia. Olympia, Archaeological Museum.*

*Perseus saves the beautiful Andromeda, the daughter of Cassiopeia, queen of Ethiopia, from the jaws of the ferocious sea-monster Ketos. Drawing after a black-figure Corinthian amphora painted c. 560 B.C. Berlin, Staatliche Museen: inv. no. F 1637.*

nymphs of the sea, Poseidon sent an enormous and voracious sea monster at their request to molest the coast of Ethiopia. The only way to rid the country of this plague was to sacrifice the princess Andromeda, to the monster. It was while she was chained naked to the rocks to await her fate that Perseus fell instantly in love with her. After hasty consultation with her father Cepheus, Perseus agreed to save her on condition that she was granted to him in marriage. And so it was.

# BELLEROPHON AND THE CHIMAERA

T he son of Glaucus, king of Corinth, Bellerophon had involuntarily killed a man by the name of Bellerus, perhaps a tyrant of Corinth (Bellerophontes meaning the "killer of Bellerus"). To expiate this crime Bellerophon was obliged to seek exile in Tiryns at the court of King Proetus, who purified him of his guilt. The king's wife Steneboea was strongly attracted to the handsome and noble appearance of the youth who rejected her advances out of loyalty to the king. The enraged and humiliated Steneboea in revenge made Proetus believe that Bellerophon had attempted to violate her. Proetus decided to send the hero to the court of Iobates, Steneboea's father in Lycia, accompanied by a letter, requesting that its bearer be put to death. Iobates then charged Bellerophon with the seemingly impossible task of killing the Chimaera. This monster, the daughter of Typhon and Echidna ("the viper") had the body and head of a lion, spitting fire, from whose shoulders grew the head of a goat with a serpent as its tail. Bellerophon received the invaluable help of Athene who presented him with a magic bridle with which to capture and tame the winged horse Pegasus, the son of Medusa, who he had surprised drinking at the Peirene spring in Corinth. Flying high above his victim Bellerophon succeeded in killing the Chimaera and escaped the mortal blows from her head; according to another tradition Bellerophon thrust a lump of lead into her mouth with the point of his spear which, melting in the flames, consumed her insides and killed her.

*Bellerophon, on the winged horse Pegasus, attempts to spear the monstrous Chimaera. Drawing after a black-figure Corinthian aryballos (perfume vase) of c. 650 B.C. discovered at Thebes. Boston, Museum of Fine Arts: inv. no. 400.*

*Etruscan gilt clasp decorated with Pegasus, the winged horse c. 530 B.C.* Rome, National Etruscan Museum, Villa Giulia: inv. no. 53865.

Corinth: the Peirene spring. Large public source of water reflecting a variety of architectural phases, built beside the agora, or main square, on the road to the sea. According to tradition the winged horse Pegasus, son of the monstrous Gorgon, was surprised here, while drinking the fresh spring water, by Bellerophon, the son of Glaucus, king of Corinth, who then captured and tamed him.

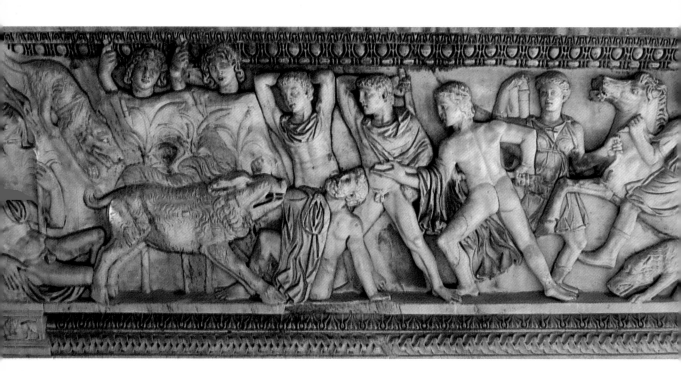

*Meleager and Atalanta, together with the noblest heroes in Greece, take part in the hunt of the fierce Calydonian Boar. Detail of a Roman sarcophagus showing the boar wounding the hero Ancius (2nd century A.D.).*

# MELEAGER, ATALANTA AND THE CALYDONIAN BOAR

Oeneus, king of Calydon, a city in Aetolia, had enjoyed a particularly fruitful harvest and abundance of crops and had made sacrificial offerings as a sign of his gratitude to all the gods, but by an oversight omitted Artemis. In revenge the goddess sent an enormous boar to devastate the land and kill her countrymen. Meleager, the king's son by Althea, decided to organise a hunt against the boar and summoned the noblest heroes from throughout Greece to his aid: the Dioscuri, Castor and Polydeuces, Theseus, Jason, Iphicles, Pirithous, Telamon, Peleus and Amphiaraus all took part. Atalanta was the only woman allowed to participate in such an heroic and sporting activity, generally reserved to men.

Atalanta, who was born in Arcadia, had grown up to excel in all sports and even refused matrimony to those unable to defeat her in a running race, which she always won. Only Melanion gained victory over Atalanta by letting fall the golden apples from the garden of the Hesperides, given him by Aphrodite. These the young maiden stopped to pick up allowing Melanion time to win the race and gain her as his bride. Atalanta was however recognised as the equal of men in heroic valour for her defeat of so many rivals.

Before leaving for the chase Meleager, certain of success had promised to give the head and skin of the boar to his mother Althea on his return. Having fallen in love with Atalanta during the hunt it was to her he presented the animal's remains. Althaea then sought her revenge. On the birth of Meleager she had been presented with a burning brand by the Moirae, or Fates, with the promise that the child would live until the brand were consumed by the fire. The mother had quickly extinguished the flame and hidden the brand secretly. In her anger she now withdrew the stick and threw it on the fire where it quickly burned away and Meleager, ignorant of the prophecy, died of an instant. His sisters, cried and lamented so piteously that Artemis was moved to pity and transformed them into birds, called Meleagrides (guineahens) by the ancient Greeks.

# OEDIPUS, THE SPHINX
# AND THE INELUCTABLE POWER OF FATE

Laius, king of Thebes of the seven gates, had been informed by an oracle of his death by the hand of his own son and so when his wife Jocasta bore him a child Laius ordered his removal from the city and his murder. The servant given this dreadful charge failed to perform it however and left the baby exposed on Mount Cithaeron with his feet bound together. The child was discovered by Periboea, queen of Corinth and the wife of Polybus, who took him and brought him up as her own, calling him Oedipus on account of his bound and therefore deformed feet. Eventually Oedipus was informed, also by an oracle, that his destiny was to kill his own father. Horrified at this idea, and confident that he was the son of Polybus, Oedipus fled to Thebes where on a narrow stretch of road he ran into Laius in his chariot and was ordered by the royal charioteer to stand aside. In the violent exchange which followed Oedipus killed both Laius and his charioteer. He continued towards Thebes, ignorant of his fulfilment of the first half of the prophecy, and came across the Sphinx at the city gates. The monstrous creature had a lion's body with the head of a woman which uttered mysterious riddles to passers-by and devoured all those without the answers. Her favourite question was "which creature walks on four legs in the morning, two at midday, and three in the evening?" Oedipus supplied the correct answer: man, who crawls when an infant, walks upright in his prime, and in old age requires the help of a stick. The disappointed Sphinx hurled herself from the high rocks where she had perched for so long.

*Oedipus is asked a mysterious riddle by the Sphinx at the gates of Thebes. Inside of a red-figure Attic cup by the painter known as the Painter of Oedipus, c. 480 B.C. Rome, Vatican Museums.*

His arrival in Thebes met with a triumphant welcome from its citizens, who were heartily weary of the Sphinx's ill treatment. He was also greeted enthusiastically at court and given to Jocasta in marriage. After many years and the birth of four children, Antigone, Ismene, Eteocles and Polynices, a terrible plague descended on the city. The cause, according to the blind sage, Tiresias, was the incestuous and immoral behaviour of the royal family. After careful enquiry the truth of Tiresias's allegation was made clear, driving Jocasta to suicide and Oedipus to blind himself with one of her pins and quit the city, his sole companion in exile being his daughter Antigone.

His guilt had repercussions for generations: Eteocles and Polynices fought over the throne and lead the city into war. Six heroes from throughout Greece were engaged on the side of Polynices, "the Seven against Thebes", one at each of the city gates, come to reclaim the throne from Eteocles, who failed to relinquish it as agreed at the end of the first year. When these

brothers killed each other the throne passed to Creon, the brother of Jocasta, who gave ceremonial burial to Eteocles but denied it to Polynices. Antigone, in torment as whether to obey human or divine law, gave her brother symbolic burial by throwing a handful of earth on his exposed body and so committed a capital offence. Ismene, fell in love with a young Theban whom she arranged to meet secretly by a spring, where spied upon by the violent Tydeus, she too was slain.

# CHAPTER IV

# THE ILIAD: THE TROJAN WAR

## THE WEDDING OF PELEUS AND THETIS

The marriage between Peleus, king of Phthia, in Thessaly, and the sea-nymph Thetis (the daughter of Nereus and therefore one of the Nereids) brought forth Achilles, the most celebrated hero of the Trojan war, and it was this semi-divine union which was the real prelude to the conflict.

At the splendid nuptial celebrations on Mount Pelius, during which the Muses themselves sang the epithalamium, all the gods in attendance presented a rich array of gifts: among the most prized were an ash-wood spear from the centaur Chiron, who was to become Achilles's mentor; two immortal horses Balius and Xanthus from Poseidon, which later played their part in the war yoked to Achilles chariot. The festivities were marred however by the appearance of Eris (Discordia), angered at her exclusion from the festivities, who threw down an golden apple inscribed with "For the Fairest", the apple of Discord, fiercely contested by Athene, Hera and Aphrodite. The dispute became increasingly bitter with no guest willing to award victory to any candidate for fear of offending the others. At the suggestion of Zeus, Hermes led the three goddesses to Mount Ida where Paris was to settle the contest.

## THE JUDGEMENT OF PARIS

When Paris, the son of Hecuba and Priam, king of Troy, saw the three goddesses arrive on Mount Ida, where he was watching sheep, he was dazzled and tried to flee. Hermes reassured him that he had nothing to fear as he had been chosen by Zeus to judge the rival claims of Athene, Aphrodite and Hera. He listened carefully to all three: each promised him extravagant gifts in return for the coveted golden apple. Athene offered wisdom and victory in war; Hera, power and sovereignty over all Asia; Aphrodite, the love of the most beautiful woman on earth, Helen of Sparta, whose beauty was famed throughout the known world. Without any hesitation Paris presented the apple to the goddess of love.

Helen was the daughter of Zeus and Leda and therefore the sister of the Dioscuri, Cas-

*One of the great bronze statues of the 4th century B.C. recently discovered at Piraeus, the port of Athens, has been identified as the young Trojan prince, Paris. He was called upon to judge the fairest of the goddesses and is shown here offering the apple ( now lost, but probably made of gold) to Aphrodite as a sign of victory. In exchange the goddess of love promised Paris the love of Helen of Troy, the most beautiful of mortal women, a gift which gave occasion to the Trojan war.*
*Piraeus, Archaeological Museum.*

*Etruscan bronze mirror (3rd century B.C) depicting the Judgement of Paris.*
*Rome, National Etruscan Museum, Villa Giulia.*

*The Greek ambassadors in Troy attempt to reclaim Helen after she has been carried away by Paris. Drawing after an embossed bronze tripod, c. 620 B.C. from the sanctuary of Zeus at Olympia. Olympia, Archaeological Museum: inv. no. B 3600.*

tor and Pollux, and of Clytemnestra (who later played an important role in the ensuing wars); she was captivated by the youth and beauty of Paris, and consented to leave Sparta with him when he returned to Troy. She took much Spartan treasure with her, and a plentiful quantity of servants, but abandoned her only daughter, Hermione, the child of her lawful husband Menelaus, the son of Atreus and king of Sparta.

When Helen was still at the court of her foster-father Tyndareus and besieged by numerous suitors, to avoid foreseeable quarrels it was decided that each suitor would make a solemn oath to defend her chosen husband against any who resented his good fortune and rightful possession. It was this promise by so many valiant princes which made Helen's betrayal of Menelaus a matter of state leading to a war in which all the rulers of Greece were engaged.

After the elopement of Paris and Helen, it was first decided to send an ambassador from Greece to Troy to demand the return of Helen to her rightful husband. But all diplomatic efforts to resolve the matter peacefully proved vain, and war became inevitable.

*Menelaus, after his entry into Troy in the wooden horse, reclaims his beautiful wife, Helen, by force, as Paris runs away in fear. Black-figure Attic amphora, painted c. 540 B.C. Rome, Vatican Museums.*

# ACHILLES AT SCYROS

Heralds were sent throughout Greece to summon volunteers for the expedition to Troy, in Asia. As an oracle had revealed to Peleus, or according to others to Thetis, that his son would die beneath the walls of Troy, Achilles was disguised as a girl and sent to the court of King Lycomedes at Scyros, where he lived for nine years among Lycomedes's daughters under the pseudonym Pyrrha, on account of his auburn hair. Achilles's union with one of the daughters, Deidameia, resulted in the birth of Pyrrhus, later called Neoptolemus, who also took part in the long war against Troy after the death of Achilles.

Pelide (the son of Peleus) could not however escape his destiny. Ulysses, mindful of the prophecy of the seer Calchas that Troy could not by taken without the aid of the young Achilles, set out in search of him and arrived at the court of Lycomedes dressed as a merchant. When he spread his precious wares before all the women of the court they were immediately attracted by his costly fabrics and embroideries while "Pyrrha" lighted on some rare weapons hidden by Ulysses in the pile. His true identity thus revealed, Achilles could no longer remain in hiding and Peleus and Thetis could no longer oppose his departure for the war.

# THE SACRIFICE OF IPHIGENIA
## AND THE DEPARTURE FOR TROY

Having first gathered at Argo, in the kingdom of Agamemnon, commander of the Greek forces, the ships dropped anchor at Aulis, their progress halted for lack of a wind. Calchas was again consulted and explained that they were becalmed at the will of Artemis who had been angered by Agamemnon. Some sources suggest that he had been negligent in her regard, either by killing a deer, an animal sacred to the goddess, and boasting that Artemis herself could not have done better, or because Agamemnon's father Atreus had withheld a golden lamb from the goddess, and, as was the rule in antiquity, his guilt had passed to his son, or else because Agamemnon was stained with perjury. He had promised to sacrifice the finest new born creature to Artemis in the year his daughter Iphigenia had been born, and had failed to do so. Whatever the cause of Artemis's anger, Calchas revealed that the only way to appease the goddess was by the sacrifice of Iphigenia. Agamemnon, spurred by his own ambition and urged on by his companions, especially by Ulysses and Menelaus, was now unable to save his daughter.

Iphigenia was in Argo with her mother Clytemnestra when they received a message from Agamemnon ordering her immediate departure for Aulis, where she was to be married to Achilles before the departure of the fleet. Iphigenia arrived obedient to her father's summons, and was sacrificed to Artemis at the hand of Calchas. But according to some, the goddess was moved with pity at the last minute, and substituting a fawn for the maiden, brought her safely to Tauris, where she became one of her priestesses.

# THE SIEGE OF TROY

With favourable winds the Greek fleet at last set sail and eventually reached the Troad, dropping anchor at the island of Tenedos.

The Greeks were encamped for nine years outside the walls of Troy (now in Turkey, at the mouth of the Dardanelles) before the unfolding of those events related in the Iliad. Various accounts, written for the most part later than the great Homeric poem, relate the skirmishes which took place during the first nine years. They consist mainly of pirate raids and the plunder of the islands and surrounding cities of Asia Minor. Notable among these episodes is the capture of Hypoplacian Thebes by Achilles (Cryseis was taken in the plunder of the city and later presented to Agamemnon), and the expedition against Lyrnessus, where Achilles took the fair Briseis captive.

The most celebrated conflicts involving the direct engagement of the both armies were those immediately after the landing of the Greeks, in which victory went to the Trojans. Later, however, after Achilles had killed Cycnus, the son of Poseidon, the tide turned against the Trojans and they were forced to retreat inside the city walls.

# THE DEATH OF TROILIUS

There is another event which belongs to the early stages of the war, narrated with considerable detail and given importance but only by sources later than Homer, an event determining the final victory of the Greeks.

According to the prophecy of a celebrated oracle, Troy could not be captured if Troilius the youngest son of Priam and Hecuba, or according to another tradition of Apollo and Hecuba, reached the age of twenty.

As it happened shortly after the Greeks encamped outside the city Troilius was killed by Achilles who had prepared an ambush near the spring where the young prince would go to water his horses, often in the company of his sister Polyxena who would refresh herself with the cool waters.

*Achilles waits in ambush behind the fountain where Troilius goes to water his horse. Etruscan painting, 6th century B.C. Tarquinia, Tomb of the Tori.*

## THE WRATH OF ACHILLES

The events narrated in the Homeric poem only begin in the tenth year of the war and open with the dispute between Achilles and Agamemnon over the possession of Briseis the slave-girl.

As the Greek forces were severely afflicted by a terrible plague the seer, Calchas, was summoned once again for advice. He revealed that the scourge was a manifestation of the anger of Apollo and had been inflicted on them by the intervention of his priest Chryses, whose daughter Chryseis had been captured during the siege of Thebes and assigned to Agamemnon as booty. Achilles summoned a council of all the Greek leaders which resulted in the decision to restore Chryseis to her father. Agamemnon agreed to bide by the decision on condition that Briseis, the young slave kept by Achilles, was given to him in exchange. Achilles withdrew to his tent angered at the injustice of the request, refusing to participate further in the conflict until Agamem-

non could justify his claim. When Agamemnon's heralds came to claim Briseis, Achilles handed her over but,
deeply offended, went to the water's edge and invoked the
name of his mother Thetis. Thetis knew full well that the
Greeks would not gain victory over the Trojans until Achilles
joined in the battle, and so she advised her son to allow the Trojans to attack the Greeks, even letting them advance as far as the
ships. When the situation became untenable Agamemnon would
be forced to come to terms with Achilles. Furthermore, Thetis
interceded for her son with Zeus, who agreed to give the Trojans the upper hand for as long as Achilles remained withdrawn
from the fighting.

# THE DEATH OF PATROCLUS

When the Trojans had advanced as far as the Greek ships and appeared on the point of victory, Agamemnon sent envoys to Achilles imploring him to take up arms again, promising to restore Briseis in addition to a reward of twenty of the most beautiful Trojan women and the hand of one of his daughters. The hero remained unmoved despite the supplication of his childhood friend, the faithful Patroclus, who had accompanied him on this as on many other expeditions. Even the dire account of the Greeks' plight as described by Patroclus failed to persuade Achilles to change his mind. Achilles did grant Patroclus leave to return to the battlefield himself accompanied by the Myrmidons, Achilles select body of fighters. Patroclus was also granted the use of Achilles's arms and armour, its appearance alone striking terror into the ranks of the Trojans, convinced that the great Greek hero had again lent his support to their enemy.

Patroclus threw himself into the thick of the battle, dealing death to the Trojans, and forcing them to consider withdrawal. Just as he reached Hector's chariot, where he felled Cebrion, the charioteer, Apollo intervened and, siding with Hector, guided his hand to the destruction of Patroclus.

*The funeral games organised by Achilles in honour of his faithful friend Patroclus, killed by Hector, take place before the whole army who pay homage to the valour of the fallen hero. Fragment of a black-figure dinos (globe-shaped vase for wine) signed by the great Athenian painter Sophilos (c. 580 B.C.), discovered at Pharsalos. Athens, National Archaeological Museum: inv. no. 15499.*

A dispute then arose over the body of the slain Patroclus, already stripped by the Trojans of the divine armour of Achilles, given to Achilles by his mother Thetis and forged as a wedding present from Hephaestus to Peleus. Achilles, learning of the death of his faithful Patroclus, was prostrate with grief but also furious for revenge and advanced unarmed into the enemy ranks where, with a single cry he put the Trojans to flight and had the body of his friend recovered.

In honour of Patroclus Achilles organised magnificent funeral celebrations, with all the Greek leaders participating in the traditional games, and the sacrifice of twelve young noble Trojans on the funeral pyre.

*Achilles prepares his famous horse for battle, at that moment granted the gift of prophecy and of speech. Fragment of a black-figure bowl signed by the great Athenian painter Nearkos, c.560 B.C. Athens, National Archaeological Museum: inv. no. Acr. 611.*

## THE VENGEANCE OF ACHILLES

It was the grief and anger of Achilles at the death of Patroclus which drove him back into the conflict and, having expressed his readiness to Agamemnon, he put on the new armour Thetis had had made for him by Hephaestus. As he returned to battle his horse Xanthus (the Saurian), momentarily granted the gift of prophecy, announced his imminent death. Careless of this prophecy and disdaining every danger, Achilles threw himself among the Trojans, who fled in terror. Only Aeneas, inspired by Apollo, was prepared to confront the fury of the son of Peleus but when Achilles pierced Aeneas's shield with his spear and Aeneas was intent on counterattack with an enormous rock the combatants were separated by Poseidon, who kept them both from harm by engulfing them in a cloud. Aeneas was destined for far greater things than to be slain by Achilles beneath the walls of Troy.

Hector too was eager to join in combat against Achilles, but destiny for a short time kept them apart. Achilles continued his advance on Troy dividing the Trojans by the river Scamander where he took numerous prisoners, later sacrificed on the tomb of Patroclus. The river-god rushed at Achilles to stop the slaughter, but Hep-

ΠΑΤΡΟΚΛ

In vengeance for the death of Patroclus Achilles kills Hector and then repeatedly drags his naked body (his arms have already been taken as plunder) around the walls of Troy and Patroclus's funeral mound. This daily outrage grieves Hector's aged father King Priam, with his white hair and beard, and his mother Hecuba, who beats her head in distress. In the foreground, the timely arrival of Iris, the winged messenger of Zeus, comes to put an end to the shameful scene. Iris was sent by Zeus to implore Achilles's mother Thetis, to intervene to prevent her son causing further outrage in his treatment of Hector's body. Drawing after a black-figure Attic hydria by a painter in the circle known as the Group of Leagros (c.510 B.C.). Boston, Museum of Fine Arts: inv. no. 63473.

haestus took the part of Achilles and dried up the waters. Achilles continued towards the city walls to try and cut off the retreating Trojans. Apollo yet again intervened to disorientate Achilles in his search for the gates.
When Achilles was again free to move against the retreating Trojans he was too late

and they had already closed the city gates to the enemy. Only Hector, despite the pleas of his father, calling to him from on top of the city walls and pulling out his hair, remained outside, eager to confront Achilles. The sight of Achilles as he approached filled even Hector with dread and he ran three times around the walls with Achilles in pursuit. In the meantime Zeus had balanced the destiny of the two heroes on the divine scales and the death of Hector had weighed more heavily. From this moment on not even Apollo could do anything to alter the fate of his favourite, the outcome further weighed against him by the intervention of Athene at the side of Achilles. Taking on the appearance of Deiphobus, one of Hector's surviving brothers, she convinced Hector that he could defeat Achilles with his brother's help. When Hector realised that he had been deceived it was already too late and he had been mortally wounded by Achilles, but did not die before predicting Achilles's approaching death and requesting that his own body be returned to his aged father.

Achilles, still angered by the death of Patroclus, ignored Hector's request and proudly exhibited the dead body of Hector. He slit the ankles and tied the corpse to the back of his chariot, dragging it around the walls before returning with it to the Greek camp. As if this were not a great enough affliction for all Trojans and above all for Hector's aged parents, Hector being their last hope of deliverance, Achilles repeated the offence each day, dragging around the walls of Troy the body of the Trojan who had killed his beloved Patroclus. After twelve days Thetis was charged by Zeus to communicate the gods' displeasure to Achilles for his failure to honour the dead. When Priam came to pay the ransom for his son's body, Achilles was moved with pity. He was also reminded of his own father whom he would never see again, and he agreed to surrender the mangled body for ceremonial burial.

## THE DEATH OF ACHILLES

The death of Hector was soon followed by that of his greatest enemy. Thetis had warned Achilles of his fate before his departure: he would fight in the Trojan war and gain immortal glory instead of the grey destiny reserved to him if he stayed at home. But his death would be an early one, he would be cut down on the completion of his great undertaking, the slaying of Hector.

There are numerous accounts of the death of Achilles: some say he was felled in the thick of the fighting by an arrow shot by Paris, but guided by Apollo, others that Paris shot him while Achilles was unarmed in an amorous encounter with Polyxena, one of the daughters of Priam and Hecuba. Others say that Achilles, deeply in love with Polyxena, asked for her in exchange for the body of Hector. The exchange was to take place in the temple of Apollo Thymbrius, not far from the gates of Troy. Here Paris hid behind the statue of the god and hit Achilles in the only vulnerable spot on his body, his heel (hence the expression "Achilles heel" used of somebody's weak spot, either physical or psychological).

Thetis, anxious for the mortality inherited by her sons from their father Peleus, submerged them in the miraculous waters of the Styx, the river of the Underworld, which would make them immortal. When it was Achilles's turn however, his mother held him firmly by the heel which remained unwetted by the waters, and it was only by attacking this one vulnerable spot that Paris was able to slay the hero.

## THE CONTEST FOR THE ARMS OF ACHILLES
## AND THE SUICIDE OF AJAX

Ajax, the son of Telamon and king of Salamis, had brought twelve ships to engage in the expedition against Troy. He was second only to Achilles in courage and skill at arms.

And so after the death of Achilles, when Thetis announced that his armour would go to the most courageous of the Greeks, to him who inspired most terror in the ranks of the Trojans, Ajax was convinced that they would be allotted to him. When the Trojan prisoners were asked who they most feared, they in disrespect named Odysseus, instead of Ajax. Denied his rightful prize, Ajax grew mad at the offence and slaughtered much of the livestock intended to feed the Greeks, which in his madness he mistook for the Achaean leaders. In the morning when he recovered enough to realise what he had done, he threw himself on his own sword in shame and sorrow.

*Ajax places his sword in the ground in preparation for his suicide. He has suffered the shame of Agamemnon not granting him the arms of Achilles after the death of the hero in battle. Drawing after a black-figure amphora by the great Athenian painter Exekias (c. 540 B.C.).* Boulogne-sur-Seine, Museum: inv. 558.

# CASSANDRA, LAOCOON AND THE TROJAN HORSE

When the Greeks, after ten years of war in which victory appeared certain first for one side and then for the other, no longer knew what strategy to adopt to secure victory and return home, the brilliant and cunning Odysseus came to their aid. The ruler of Ithaca devised a way of attacking the city from within, hiding warriors inside the famous wooden horse. The Trojans themselves would drag the horse into Troy, believing it an offering pleasing to Athene, and then the Greeks would cut them down in their sleep. To make events appear more plausible, as recounted to the Trojans by the Greek Sinon, who pretended to be a traitor, the Achaeans burnt their camp and withdrew in their ships to the island of Tenedos, not visible from Troy.

When the Trojans saw the horse and Sinon explained that it had been left as a propitiatory offering to the goddess Athene to speed the Greeks on their return journey, and that it had been built so large to prevent the Trojans dragging it into their own city to use themselves as an offering, the Trojans rejoiced and gave thanks in the belief that they had seen the last of their enemies. They also set about inventing a scheme, involving the destruction of part of their ramparts, to bring the wonderful horse into the city.

Not all Trojans shared in the celebrations nor trusted in the good faith of the Greeks and of Sinon. Most vehement in argument against bringing the horse within the walls was Cassandra, one of the daughters of Priam and Hecuba, and Laocoon, the priest of Apollo also urged strongly against it.

While the horse still stood on the beach Laocoon took a spear from one of the warriors and hurled it against the body of the horse. Despite the hollow sound nobody listened to his warning to put the Trojans on guard as the horse was sure to be some treacherous invention of cunning Odysseus.

Nor was Cassandra believed. She had been granted the gift of prophecy by Apollo in the expectation of receiving her favours. Once she had learnt the art of divination

*Facing page: Laocoon, who had warned the Trojans against introducing the wooden horse into the city, and his sons are crushed by serpents sent by Apollo. Monumental sculptural group by Hagesandros, Polydoros and Athanadoros of Rhodes, c. 50 B.C. Copy of a bronze original of 140-139 B.C. Rome, Vatican Museums: inv. nos. 1059, 1064, 1067.*

*The Trojan horse. Detail of a fresco from a house in Pompeii (c. 70 A.D.).* Naples, Archaeological Museum.

*The fully-armed Greek soldiers emerge from the wooden horse at dead of night (note the wheels providing mobility!). As a result of Odysseus's cunning plan the Greeks succeeded in penetrating Troy after a ten-year siege and proceeded to sack and destroy the city. Drawing after the decoration on the neck of a pithos (large earthenware jar) with relief decoration produced in the Cyclades, probably on the island of Tinos (c. 670 B.C.). Mykonos, Archaeological Museum: inv. no. 2240.*

Cassandra refused to keep her part of the bargain therefore incurred Apollo's anger. She was allowed to keep her prophetic gift but was doomed never to be believed. Therefore although she unveiled the dark truth about the horse, she was ignored just as she had been on previous occasions during the war. When Paris first made his return to the city in disguise she announced that he would cause the downfall of Troy and its inhabitants. When he later reappeared accompanied by Helen, Cassandra announced that the abduction of the wife of Menelaus would cause their destruction.

Laocoon's fate was even more unhappy. Scorned by his people he hurried to the water's edge to offer a bull in sacrifice to Poseidon in order to bring down a storm on the Greek fleet. As he reached the shore he saw two monstrous sea serpents emerge from the water and entangle themselves around his two sons. He ran in desperation to their assistance but he too was enveloped in their fatal coils and crushed to death. The Trojans interpreted this as Laocoon's punishment for his want of respect to the goddess Athene when he had hurled the spear against her sacrificial horse. It was in fact a punishment sent by Apollo, angered by the priest who had once profaned his temple by coupling with his wife right behind the statue of the god. The Trojans knew nothing of this however and the horse was dragged into the city.

# THE DESTRUCTION OF THE CITY

The day the Trojans believed the Greeks to have departed was a day of jubilation and, after destroying a section of the wall, they pulled the wooden horse into the heart of Troy. The rest of the day and most of the night was spent in drinking, feasting and celebration. With the city sleeping deeply all around him Sinon climbed onto the ramparts with a flare to signal to the ships anchored off Tenedos. He then returned to the wooden horse and released the hidden warriors who immediately dispersed throughout the city, bringing death and destruction to the city and its citizens. The Trojans, still suffering from their heady celebrations, responded to the surprise attack as best they could, hurling spits, table implements and even the flaming beams and rafters from their own houses against the enemy. But they were powerless in the face of the fury and cruelty of the Greeks, ten years away from their homeland and exacerbated by the long weary years of war. Neoptolemus, the young son of Achilles, slaughtered the aged King Priam who had taken shelter near an altar raised to Zeus. Hector's son Astyanax was wrenched from the arms of his mother Andromache and flung over the city walls to his death. The young Ajax, the son of Oïleus, dragged Cassandra piteously from the temple of Athene, where she had taken refuge, and ignominiously tore her garments. There was nothing now that Athene could do to help her priestess or the city; the fate of Troy was sealed.

*Ajax violates Cassandra: a dramatic episode in the destruction of Troy (Illiouperis). The Greek hero Ajax, son of Oïleus, succeeded in entering the palace at Troy to find Cassandra hidden in the shrine of Athene. Marble vase with relief decoration, known as the "Medici Krater" (Augustan era). Florence, Uffizi Gallery.*

*Gold leaf funeral mask, known as the Mask of Agamemnon, discovered by Heinrich Schliemann in a tomb in the great circle of Mycenae. Athens, National Archaeological Museum.*

When it was clear that nothing more could be done to save Troy, courageous Aeneas took his aged father Anchises on his shoulders and led his wife Creusa and his son Ascanius from the city. He escaped under the protection of his mother, Aphrodite, removing all the city's gods, the Penates, with him. Some say that Aphrodite had indicated that his destiny lay elsewhere, in the foundation of a city to the west, born from the ashes of Troy, from where he would rule the entire world.

*Mycenae. The dromos (entrance corridor) and doorway of one of the large tombs in the acropolis, known as the Tomb of Clytemnestra.*

## THE RETURN OF AGAMEMNON

The events following the war and the destruction of Troy, are related in the Odyssey and later poems, called the "Returns". Here it is enough to give an account of Agamemnon and his family, in so far as they were affected by Agamemnon's role as commander in chief of the Greek army.

Clytemnestra remained faithful to Agamemnon until she heard of his possession of the slave-girl Chryseis. At that time Clytemnestra was being courted by the insistent young Aegisthus, whom she resisted until he banished her faithful counsellor, Demodocus, from the court. She then abandoned herself to the love of Aegisthus, who ruled as king in Argo until the return of Agamemnon.

Aegisthus posted sentinels on the shore to signal with flares when they sighted the return of Agamemnon. A sumptuous banquet was prepared, during which Aegisthus and some twenty accomplices who lay in hiding surprised Agamemnon and killed him in front of Clytemnestra.

*Mycene. The long entrance corridor to the imposing tholos tomb (central chamber covered by a dome), known as the Tomb of Agamemnon, discovered by Schliemann. The monumental tomb is considered the finest example of Mycenaean funeral architecture and has a central circular chamber covered by a vaulted roof raised 31 layers of tiles in height. A small side room housed the rich funeral objects. The tomb is covered by a mound of earth which stabilised the entire structure while the hollow triangle above the architrave was designed to lighten the weight of the roof at the opening. The tomb was enriched with door-jambs, pilasters and frames made of pietre dure with relief decoration.*

Some say that it was Clytemnestra herself who stabbed her husband having given him a robe with no openings after his bath. His body entrapped she was able to stab him without any resistance. She therefore avenged the death of Iphigenia who had been sacrificed by her father to Artemis, in order to secure a favourable wind for the departure of the Greek fleet from Aulis. Cassandra also met her fate at the hand of Clytemnestra. She was guilty in the queen's eyes for having become, willingly or not, Agamemnon's favourite slave, granted to him as part of the plunder of Troy.
The bloody history begun with the sacrifice of Iphigenia did not end until many years later when Orestes, the son of Agamemnon and Clytemnestra, returned home, from whence he had been sent as a child, to kill Clytemnestra and her lover.

*Queen Clytemnestra kills the young Cassandra, brought to Argos by Agamemnon as his war-slave and lover. Bronze relief from the sanctuary of Hera at Argos (c. 650 B.C.).* Athens, National Archaeological Museum.

*Clytemnestra and her lover Aegisthus kill Agamemnon on his return from Troy (c. 630 B.C.). Earthenware votive tablet from Gortyn in Crete.* Heraklion, Archaeological Museum.

*Clytemnestra kills Cassandra who tries in vain to seek refuge at an altar. Tondo inside a red-figure Attic cup painted c. 430 B.C.* Ferrara, National Archaeological Museum.

# CHAPTER V

# THE ODYSSEY: THE WANDERINGS OF ODYSSEUS

Homer's *Odyssey* is so called because it describes all Odysseus's adventures in the ten years it took him to return to Ithaca, a small island off the north-west coast of Greece.

## THE LOTUS-EATERS

The Greeks' departure from Troy was marred by a bitter quarrel between Menelaus and Agamemnon. Although Odysseus set sail with the latter, a violent storm soon drove their ships apart and Odysseus and his men were sent south by a relentless north wind which drove them onto the island of Cythera. After spending two days there they again set sail and were carried as far as the Libyan promontory, where the Lotus-eaters dwelt. Odysseus sent a few of his men ahead to explore and they were given a warm welcome by the inhabitants and offered the delicious fruit of the lotus to eat. Once this had been tasted the men lost all desire to leave the place and return home. It was only by force that Odysseus, who resisted the lotus, was able to drag the men back to the ships and set sail again.

*The blinding of the Cyclop Polyphemus by Odysseus and his companions is to be found depicted both on Greek vases (above, 650 B.C.),* Eleusis, Archaeological Museum, *as well as on Etruscan ones (below, 530 B.C.).* Rome, Etruscan Museum, Villa Giulia.

## POLYPHEMUS AND THE LAND OF THE CYCLOPS

Sailing north from Libya the heroes reached an island with an abundance of goats, with which they might provision the ships. It is usually identified with Sicily, and was the home of the Cyclops. These monstrous creatures were giants of enormous strength but with only one eye. They watched over their flocks, and although some mention the Cyclops' involvement in various myths, assisting in the fortification of various cities, they were incapable of building any themselves or of living in a sociable way. They lived rather in isolated and inhospitable caves and fed on raw, including human, flesh. When Odysseus and his men had explored for some time they went into one of the caves, belonging to the giant

Polyphemus, where Odysseus was urged by his men to take as many sheep and cheeses as they could carry and return hastily to their ships. Odysseus refused and when Polyphemus returned and discovered them in his cavern he began by eating two of the sailors for his supper. Odysseus then offered him some of his strong wine, a drink never before tasted by the Cyclops. Polyphemus became more agreeable and when he asked Odysseus his name Odysseus cunningly replied "Oudeis", meaning "Nobody" in Greek and easily confused with "Odysseus". Polyphemus then happily promised that he would save Odysseus for the last mouthful, as he had given him the wine, and having drunk another bowlful, fell into a deep sleep. Odysseus and his companions immediately took a burning stake from the fire, which they had built, and thrust it into the Cyclop's eye. Even so Polyphemus sought to prevent their escape by blocking the opening of the cave, but Odysseus tied his men under the bellies of the rams to escape Polyphemus's searching hands. When Odysseus too had escaped Polyphemus cried out with pain and frustration but the other Cyclops feared he had gone mad and did nothing to help him, for when they asked who had injured him he answered "Oudeis", "Nobody". As the ships pulled out to sea Odysseus could not resist letting Polyphemus know the true identity of his assailant and so Polyphemus realised that an ancient oracle had been fulfilled predicting his blindness at the hand of Odysseus. As a result of this incident Poseidon, the father of Polyphemus, did everything in his power to prevent Odysseus's return to his homeland.

## THE ISLAND OF AEOLUS

The surviving company then sailed on until they reached the island of Aeolus, the god of the winds, who welcomed them hospitably and gave Odysseus a leather bag containing all the winds save the favourable west one which would blow them direct to Ithaca. When they were at last in sight of home the sailors opened the bag by night believing it to contain gold, letting the winds escape in a tempest, blowing them far off course. Eventually they were forced to return to Aeolus where Odysseus asked once again for a favourable wind. The god of the winds refused his request, as it was quite evident that the gods were hostile to Odysseus's return to his homeland.

*Two of Odysseus's companions transformed into pigs by the enchantress Circe in her cave. Red-figure lekythos (funerary vase for perfume) by an Attic painter, c. 470 B.C. Athens, National Archaeological Museum: inv. no. 9685.*

# CIRCE, THE ENCHANTRESS

The men, now having little control over the direction of their course, given the obvious hostility of the gods, reached the land of the Laestrygones, peopled with cannibals, and generally believed to lie on the Italian coast between Formia and Gaeta. From there they sailed to the island of Aeaea, between Gaeta and Terracina, the home of Circe. Odysseus, fearful for the safety of his men, sent only a small contingent to explore this unknown land. They discovered a fine palace where Circe invited them to a delicious banquet. No sooner had the men eaten of the enchanted food than Circe touched them with her wand transforming them into pigs, lions and dogs, according to their temperaments. The sad fate of his companions was witnessed by Eurylochus who, fearing foul play, had watched the sad events from his hiding-place. When Eurylochus related the outcome of the feast to Odysseus the hero determined

*Odysseus threatens Circe with his sword to reveal the antidote after she had transformed his men into pigs. Scene carved on the end of a stone Etruscan sarcophagus (4th century B.C.). Orvieto, Claudio Faina Museum.*

The sirens were half-woman, half-bird with voices so melodious no man could resist them. Odysseus succeeded in hearing them, and surviving, by having his men strap him to the mast of his ship. Like the sphinxes, the Sirens belonged to the liminal world between this life and the beyond; they accompanied the spirits of the dead and might appear as funerary statuary. Marble statue of 4th century B.C. depicting one of the Sirens playing a musical instrument. Part of the funerary monument of Dexileos in the Cemetery of the Keramikos in Athens. Athens, National Archaeological Museum: inv. no. 774.

on returning to Circe's palace in an attempt to save his men. In the woods separating the beach from the palace he met Hermes who instructed him on how to escape the enchantment. He gave him a herb "moly" to be mixed with the Circe food to render it innocuous; Hermes further told him that when he then drew his sword on Circe she would surrender totally to the hero's power. All happened as Hermes predicted: Odysseus was invited to dine but mixed "moly" with his wine so that the Circe's attempt at his transformation had no effect. When Odysseus then threatened to kill Circe she swore by the Styx that she had never caused anyone harm and restored the sailors to their original forms. Odysseus spared her life and stayed a month, and some say a year, with her as her lover and she bore him sons. It was on the advice of the Circe that Odysseus made a journey to Hades, the land of the dead, to consult the spirit of the seer, Tiresias. He predicted that Odysseus would only return home alone, on a strange ship and that when he reached his own palace he would have to avenge himself on the his wife's suitors. When Odysseus finally took leave of Circe she gave him further invaluable advice help him in his coming trials.

## THE SIRENS

Leaving the promontory of Circeo, heading south, Odysseus sailed towards the gulf of Naples passing close by the island inhabited by the sirens. These terrible bird-like creatures with the heads of women were the daughters of the river-god, Achelous and the Muse Melpomene, or of Achelous and Sterope, the daughter of the king of Calydon, in Aetolia (north of Corinth).
The beauty of the Sirens' singing bewitched sailors who, seeking to approach

them, were wrecked on the rocky coast and then devoured by their temptresses. Warned in advance by Circe, Odysseus had his men fasten him to the mast of his ship so that he might hear the fatal melody without coming to harm. His men were told to plug their ears with wax and to pay no attention to the pleas of their master until well passed the island of the Sirens. As the first notes reached his ears Odysseus was overcome with desire to go to the Sirens, but his sailors ignored all his supplications and threats. The danger passed, the Sirens threw themselves onto the rocks in desperation that Odysseus had resisted their enchantment, and were never heard again.

## SCYLLA AND CHARYBDIS

Continuing on his voyage south Odysseus next encountered the perilous Scylla and Charybdis in the straits of Messina. These sea-monsters were both originally young women, transformed by the vengeance of the gods. Scylla, who lived on the mainland side of the Straits, was transformed by Circe who was jealous of Glaucus's love for the maiden. Circe mixed herbs in the spring where Scylla used to bathe whereupon six horrible dogs grew from the lower half of her body while her upper half remained intact. Horrified Scylla withdrew to a grotto on the straits where she hid herself from view but could do nothing to restrain the fierce dogs from attacking and devouring unsuspecting sea-farers who ventured too close to her cave.
Charybdis, on the other hand, had her grotto on the Sicilian side of the straits. The daughter of Mother Earth and Poseidon who in her human form had been inexhaustibly voracious, so much so that when Heracles passed her way with the cattle of Geryon she stole them and ate them all. Angered by her greed, Zeus struck her with lightening, sending her falling into the sea, where she was changed into a monster.

Three times a day she would suck in vast quantities of sea water together with everything floating on it, including ships, in the straits near her grotto. She then expelled the water and fed on the luckless creatures strained through her teeth. Odysseus had been given wise counsel by Circe as to how to negotiate the straits to limit the damage as much as possible. Circe explained that nobody, not even a god, could escape the power of Charybdis's intake but that by keeping as close as possible to the Italian coast, where Scylla lay, the heroes would eventually reach Trinacria, or Sicily. Carybdis would indeed have swallowed the whole fleet in a single suction while Scylla's dogs would be satisfied with only six victims. While these were being devoured the fleet might progress with favourable winds as fast as possible to reach the Sicilian coast. And so it was that Odysseus, heavy of heart, followed Circe's advice and lost only six poor sailors to Scylla.

## THE CATTLE OF THE SUN-GOD

Safely ashore in Sicily, a relentless south wind blew up, forcing Odysseus and his men to stay there for sometime. The fine herds of white cattle belonging to Helius, the Sun-god, grazed on the island but Odysseus forbade his sailors to harm them in any way. Their supplies began to run scarce and the men, disregarding Odysseus warning, slaughtered some of the beasts and feasted on them. Helius, outraged at this lack of respect, turned to Zeus for help and he sent a violent storm to batter their ship no sooner had they put to sea again. The lightening sent by the god wrecked the vessel and all the sailors perished except Odysseus who took no part in the sacrifice and clung on to the broken mast. He drifted once again towards Charybdis where only his natural cunning saved him from being swallowed, and having being tossed at random for nine more days reached the island of Calypso.

## THE LOVE OF CALYPSO

Calypso, ("She who lies concealed") was a nymph of extraordinary beauty, the daughter of Helius, or others say of Atlas, who lived on the island of Ogygia, generally identified with Ceuta, on the Moroccan coast, near the straits of Gibralter. She led a quiet and peaceful life, surrounded by her attendants, her days passed in spinning and weaving, lulled by the singing of the nymphs. When Odysseus was washed onto her shore she treated him with great hospitality, she fed and clothed him and became his lover. Odysseus happily passed many years with her but never forgot Ithaca and increasingly longed to return home. When it became clear to Odysseus that Calypso had no intention of letting him depart he turned to Athene who interceded for him with the father of the gods. Zeus sent his messenger, Hermes, to Calypso instructing her to release Odysseus. Sadly she supplied him with the wood necessary to build a raft, with food and clothing and with advice on how to read the stars and navigate home and then bade farewell to the man she loved so dearly and who had given her a son.

# Nausicaa and the Island of the Phaeacians

No sooner was Odysseus at sea again, and sailing east, than another tempest toppled him from his raft and he was only saved by his powerful swimming. At last, exhausted and naked, he was washed ashore on the island of the Phaeacians, called Scheria in the *Odyssey*, and usually identified with Corfu. Here, he crawled into a wood and lay down at the edge of a river and fell asleep. He was awoken by the shouts and laughter of a group of young girls among them Nausicaa, the lovely daughter of Alcinous, king of the Phaeacians. Their meeting had been planned by Athene so that Nausicaa might intercede for the hero at the court of her father. The goddess had sent her a dream in which her companions reproved her for her negligence and told her to go in all haste to the river to wash her clothes and those of the whole family in

preparation for her wedding. Odysseus, awakened by their cries covered his nakedness with branches, and walked towards the girls who ran away affrighted. Only Nausicaa remained and indeed was critical of her companions for ignoring the demands of hospitality towards those sent by the gods. Odysseus spoke to her softly and beguilingly saying that he had mistaken her for a goddess or a nymph on account of her great loveliness. She, eager to help him, returned with him in the evening to the city and directed his steps towards the palace.

Odysseus was welcomed warmly, a feast was prepared in his honour, he recounted his adventures to the delight of all present and was even offered the hand of Nausicaa, who was quite overcome by the splendid hero. He was obliged to refuse her hand, having a wife in Ithaca, but the hospitable Phaeacians helped him still further by providing him with a ship and crew to carry him home where they left him on a sheltered side of the island. The Phaeacians then suffered cruelly for their service at

*Penelope weaves the shroud for her father-in-law Laertes, but undoes by night all she has woven by day. With this ploy Penelope manages to postpone her choice of one of the suitors to succeed Odysseus as her husband and king for a considerable length of time. Her son, Telemachus, is depicted beside her. Scene on a red-figure Attic skyphos from Chiusi, painted by the Painter of Penelope, c. 440 B.C. (The scene on the other side of the vase is reproduced on page 113). Chiusi, National Archaeological Museum: inv. no. 1831.*

the hand of Poseidon who wrecked their ship, and surrounded their island with massive mountains so that this commercial and seafaring people could no longer use their port, the source of their well-being.

# THE RETURN TO ITHACA

Twenty years have passed (ten at war, and ten on the journey home) since Odysseus departed for Troy: time and the dangers he has undergone have so transformed his appearance that none of his fellow countrymen are able to recognise their king. Grateful for this deception, Odysseus decides to keep his identity hidden and goes first to his swineherd Eumaeus, the most faithful of his servants. He makes himself known to him and with his help meets secretly with his son Telemachus whom he had left as an infant. Odysseus, disguised as a beggar, then goes to the palace with Telemachus where nobody recognises the hero apart from his dog, Argus, and his old nurse, Euryclea.

Argus, well over twenty and full of aches and pains, rises at the sight of his old master, walks around him wagging his tail but his heart bursts, unable to bear the strain of this longed for happiness, and he dies at Odysseus's feet. It is only later that the "beggar" is recognised by Euryclea when she washes his feet in the traditional welcome to guests. The true identity of the stranger is revealed by the scar on his foot inflicted during a boar hunt at Delphi when Odysseus was a young man. Euryclea was sworn to keep the arrival of her master secret, and she kept her word. Telemachus in the meantime, acting on his father's wishes, had secured all the weapons in the palace in a single room while Odysseus appeared before the suitors, asking for something to eat. They jeered at him, especially another beggar,

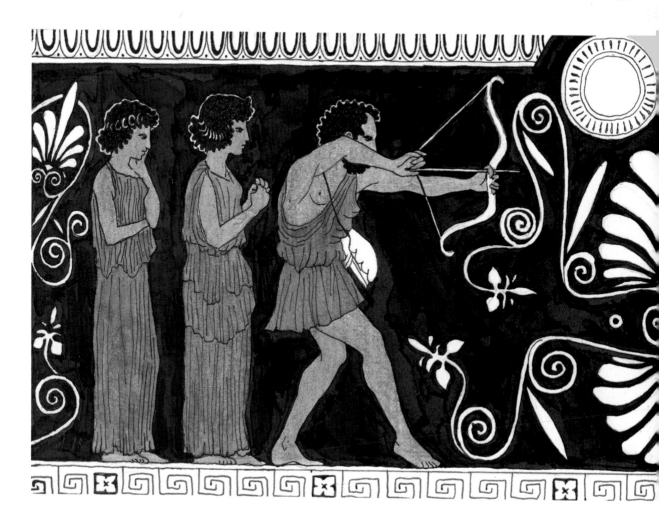

nicknamed "Irus", a favourite of the suitors, who was eager to be rid of any rival claimant to charity from the palace. Odysseus dispatched the old beggar without further ado, increasing the animosity of the suitors still further. Penelope, still ignorant of her husband's return, is now curious to meet the strange beggar from abroad to ask if he has any news of Odysseus. Odysseus, while hinting at the possibility of the hero's return, postpones the disclosure of his identity until the evening.

## PENELOPE AND THE SUITORS

When Odysseus departed for Troy he entrusted the care of his wife and estate to his old and trusted friend, Mentor: so faithful was he that sometimes Athene assumed his guise when she sought to assist Odysseus against the suitors or when she accompanied Telemachus on his journey in search of his father. Penelope alone had control of her husband's wealth.

Odysseus's mother, Anticlea, died of sorrow shortly after his departure, knowing her son to be far away and exposed to the dangers of war, while Odysseus's father, Laertes, withdrew to a life in the fields. Penelope became the focus of insistent demands for remarriage: all the young men from the surrounding contradas of Dulichio, Same, Zacynthus, as well as from Ithaca and from those cities over which Odysseus exercised sovereignty, sought her hand, eager to gain control over the kingdom's domains and riches, and these young men were known as the Suitors.

As their proposals met with the continued refusal by Penelope, they established themselves in the palace, acting as lords and wasting away Odysseus's wealth in continuous feasting and revels, hoping to bring pressure on Penelope to make a de-

*Odysseus, alone of all the company, is able to draw the bow with which he begins his elimination of the suitors who have wooed Penelope and laid claim to the throne of Ithaca in his absence. Drawing after a red-figure Attic skyphos from Tarquinia painted by the Painter of Penelope (c. 440 B.C.). Berlin, Staatliche Museen: inv. no. F 2588.*

*Delphi, the sanctuary of the Pythian Apollo is constantly referred to in the myths. The great temple dedicated to Apollo, an imposing Doric structure supported by a massive terrace wall with large polygonal blocks (510 B.C.).*

cision. Penelope reproved them severely for their behaviour to no avail; she was obliged to tolerate their continued presence in obedience to the sacred laws of hospitality. When she found she could fob them off no longer she invented the famous ruse of the weaving of the tapestry, telling them she would make her choice from among them when she had finished the tapestry, or shroud, for Laertes. And so for three years she undid by night that which she had woven by day hoping that the return of Odysseus, to whom she had remained faithful, would put an end to her difficulties. One of her one servant girls revealed her secret and forced her into the unwelcome position of having to choose from among the suitors.

Just as Odysseus arrived at the palace she presented them with a competition which she promised would prove decisive. The suitors were obliged to string Odysseus's bow and shoot his arrow through a series of axe-heads. Not one could even manage to string the great bow although Odysseus did it with ease at the first attempt.

## ODYSSEUS REGAINS HIS KINGDOM

At this point Telemachus ordered the closing of the palace doors so that the suitors, whom he had already deprived of their weapons, were at the mercy of Odysseus and his son. Those servant girls who had favoured the suitors were also punished: after they had cleared the room of the slaughtered bodies and washed away the blood, Odysseus ordered them to be hanged. It is at this point, with the suitors eliminated and his identity and regal claims fully recognised, that Odysseus revealed himself to his wife, removing any of Penelope's lingering doubts by disclosing details about their wedding chamber known only to themselves. The morning after Odysseus went to the country to meet his father and made himself known to him straight away. In the meantime the enraged relatives of the dead suitors gathered in strength to storm the palace but the intervention of Athene, once again in the guise of Mentor, foiled their attempts at revenge and peace was finally restored to Ithaca.

# CHAPTER VI

# AENEAS: FROM TROY TO ROME

*Aeneas carries his weak and aged father, Anchises, on his back and leads his small son Ascanius from the burning city of Troy on the night the Greeks managed finally to breach the city walls. It was the cunning Odysseus who thought of introducing the Greek warriors into impenetrable Troy inside the wooden horse. Aeneas's flight and the ashes of Priam's glorious city gave rise to the glory of Rome. Drawing after a black-figure Attic amphora (c. 510 B.C.). Würzburg, Martin von Wagner Museum der Universität: inv. no. 218.*

# THE HERO'S DIVINE ORIGIN

Aeneas, the son of Anchises, the Trojan prince descended from Dardanus, was also closely related to Zeus, as his mother was the goddess Aphrodite. She fell in love with Anchises while he tended his father's cattle in the mountains of the Troad. Aeneas was a brave warrior and in the Trojan army was considered second only in valour to Hector, engaging in several exchanges with the Greeks under the walls of Troy. He fought with Achilles, but was forced to retreat given the strength of his opponent, then with Diomedes who wounded him, provoking the immediate intervention of Aphrodite. In her attempt to save her son she was herself wounded so that the battle continued until Apollo withdrew Aeneas from the field, hiding him in a cloud. A cloud was later used by Poseidon to rescue the hero from a further exchange with Achilles, after the death of Patroclus, and after Aeneas had killed large numbers of Greeks.

It is quite evident from the earliest Homeric verses that Aeneas was a hero who enjoyed the special protection of the gods whom he obeyed with respect and devotion. It is equally clear that a great destiny awaited him: in him are vested all the future hopes of the royal house of Troy, hopes expressed in his mother's prophecy when she revealed her true identity to Anchises who had believed his lover to be a mere mortal. Aphrodite predicted that their union would bring forth a son who would ensure the survival of the Trojan line for countless centuries.

All these elements were later adopted by the great Latin poet, Virgil, in his epic the *Aeneid* and then interpreted in the legend surrounding Rome as the heir to the powerful Trojan dynasty and to its historic grandeur.

## THE FLIGHT FROM TROY

Once the Greeks had made their treacherous entry into Troy in the wooden horse they began their slaughter of the Trojans and the burning of the city. Aeneas, realising all was lost, lifted his aged father, Anchises, onto his back and led his wife Creusa, and young son Ascanius, away from Troy, carrying the city's gods, the Penates, together with a statue of the goddess, Pallas Athene, known as the Palladium, with him. When he reached nearby Mount Ida (it bears the same name as the one on Crete), he founded a city but did not settle there for long. He sailed with a fleet of twenty ships towards Delos, where he wanted to consult the oracle of Apollo about his own and his compatriots' future. He was told to search out the Trojans' country of origin and decided to sail on to Crete, the island which gave birth to Teucer, one of the earliest of the Trojan kings. During the night however the Penates appeared to him, instructing him to travel further to Italy, the ancient homeland of his people.

*Crete, the gulf of Haghios Nikolaus (St Nicholas), on the northern side of the island. According to legend the dynasty of the Trojan Aeneas originated in Crete and the hero landed here on his voyage towards a glorious new destiny, the birth of Rome.*

# THE JOURNEY WEST

Aeneas then continued his journey towards Esperia, the Western Mediterranean, but many difficulties were encountered before he reached his destination. A violent storm drove him onto the Strophades Islands, where the food prepared by the exhausted crew was devoured by the loathsome Harpies, half woman and half bird. They next took refuge in Epirus where they were entertained by Helenus, one of the Trojan princes, who had married Hector's widow Andromache. Once in the Ionian sea they sailed around the coast of Southern Italy but had trouble with the various Greek settlements there and decided to circumnavigate the whole of Sicily rather than sail through the perilous Straits of Messina, watched over by Scylla, a monster whose lower half was made up of six ferocious dogs which fed on passing seafarers, on the Calabrian coast, and Charybdis, a monster who took in huge quantities of sea water and all that sailed on it three times a day, on the Sicilian side.

In Sicily Aeneas and his men received a warm welcome and heard how other Trojan exiles, fleeing from the war, had been welcomed before them. Some of these, such as Aegisthus, had stayed on to become rulers over Sicilian cities. It was while they were in Sicily that Anchises, much weakened by their journey, died and was buried at Drepanum (Trapani) by Aeneas.

# DIDO AND AENEAS

When Aeneas put to sea his fleet was again tormented by a raging storm which dispersed a number of ships and sent him to Libya, where the beautiful Phoenician queen, Dido, reigned from her capital at Carthage. She fell deeply in love with Aeneas and yearned for him to remain with her as her consort. Zeus, however, did not want Aeneas to find peace and happiness in that city, destined to become the most powerful and bitter of Rome's enemies, and the hero was compelled to direct his attention once more towards Italy. The abandoned Dido, in her despair, stabbed herself with Aeneas's sword and fell on the embers of the pyre which had already destroyed Aeneas's belongings.

*The Harpies, monstrous bird-women, tormented Phineus, king of Thrace, fouling his table every time he prepared to dine. They were chased away by Calais and Zete, the winged sons of the north wind. As they took flight over the seas the Harpies also attacked Aeneas on his journey to Italy. Drawing after the black-figure frieze inside a cup by the Painter of Phineus (c. 530 B.C.), who worked in the Greek city of Rhegion (now Reggio Calabria, Italy).*

## Aeneas in Italy

When Aeneas reached the Cumaean shore he went straight to question the celebrated Cumaean Sibyl who recommended he descend to Avernus, the Latin equivalent of Hades, or the Underworld. Here Aeneas saw the shades of many of the dead and received details of his future and of his descendants. Returned to the land of the living Aeneas sailed on up the Italian coast, stopping to bury Ascanius's nurse, at Caieta (Gaeta), named after her, who had died on this last stage of the voyage. He carefully skirted the island of the enchantress, Circe, whose fame, increased by Odysseus's encounter, was spread throughout the Mediterranean and reached the mouth of the Tiber. He then visited Latium, ruled over by King Latinus who welcomed them most hospitably even offering Aeneas land on which to build a new city together with the hand of his daughter, Lavinia.

*Cuma, the cave of the Sibyl. As soon as Aeneas touched Italian soil he went to visit the famous Cumaean Sibyl who advised him to descend to Avernus, the Underworld, where he heard news of his future greatness.*

## The Hero on the Hills of Rome

Amata, the wife of Latinus, eager for Lavinia to marry Turnus, king of the neighbouring and warlike Rutules, induced him to make war against the Trojans. Aeneas left most of his men in the besieged camp on the coast and headed up the Tiber to the city of Pallanteum, where he asked for the help of King Evander, a Greek from Arcadia, once the guest of Anchises. Aeneas was welcomed and given the necessary reinforcements, headed by the king's own son Pallas. Aeneas then turned to the Etruscan city of Agylla (Cerveteri), where he gathered more troops and returned to the Trojan camp just in time to turn the tide against the fierce attack launched by Turnus and the Rutulean army.

*The Capitoline Wolf: the she-wolf gives suck to the twins Romulus and Remus, a potent symbol of the eternal city. Although born from the ashes of Troy, Rome remained profoundly affected by Greek history and culture in which myth was an essential and integral component.*

# THE FOUNDATION OF THE ETERNAL CITY

Virgil's poem closes with the death of Turnus and the victory of Aeneas. It does not recount the subsequent episodes leading to the foundation of Rome, the daughter of Troy. According to some historians Aeneas founded Lavinia, and fought to establish his power over the various peoples surrounding him, and this he finally achieved. He was accorded great honours by his people after his death; he was struck down by lightening.

Ascanius (also known as Iulus) founded the city of Albalonga and it was his descendent, Romulus, who was granted the good fortune to found the greatest city in the world, Rome.

# INDEX OF NAMES

## BRIEF GUIDE TO ARCHAEOLOGICAL TERMS

- Amphora: medium to large pot used for storing and transporting liquids and other comestibles.

- Arula: ara or altar, built on a small scale, even miniature.

- Crater: medium to large pot, for ceremonial use to mix water and wine (the Greeks never drank undiluted wine!)

- Dinos: large pot, shaped like a cauldron, and like the crater used for banquets and ceremonial purposes.

- Frieze: scene carved in stone, relating a narrative. Generally used as architectural decoration, running along above the architrave, on the outside of temples and other important public monuments.

- Pediment: architectural element on a Greek temple, being the triangular space on top of a building, often decorated with statues in the round.

- Hydria: medium size pot with three handles (two on either side and one at the back), for carrying water.

- Lekythos: small pot with a narrow opening for oils and ointments.

- Metope: decorative element on Doric temples, the space between the tryglyphs on the frieze sometimes decorated with carved scenes (in marble or stone) or painted (if decorated in terracotta).They mark the positioning of the beams supporting the temple roof.

- Oinochoe: Greek pot or vase for serving wine.

- Pelike: similar to an amphora but smaller.

- Pithos: large pot or vase for storing food.

- Psikter: similar to a thermos flask. Double walls separate the inner from the outer sections of the vase meant that the outer could be filled with cold water or ice to keep the liquid in the inner vase cool.

- Skyphos: similar to a cup with two side handles, used instead of a goblet.

- Stamnos: medium or large sized pot, put to the same use as the crater.

# INDEX